Tracking the Camino de Santiago de Compostela

· · • • • • • • • ·

Memories of Blisters and Blessings in Pursuit of the Headless Saint

Jean Goulden

Dedicated to
Molly and Bill

CAMINO DE SANTIAGO PILGRIMAGE ROUTE

Map Design by Thomas Yearwood

Prologue

Along the Way

Along the way you walk with sun,
Along the way you walk with rain
Along the way you pass through fields of stars
'Til morning comes again

Along the way you take the pleasure
Of your drink and daily bread
While each day you take as treasure
The trail still ahead

Everyday a little closer crossing
Golden growing land
Everyday a little stronger than you
Were when you began

Everyday a little meeker
As the fortune that you find is
The will to just continue on,
Your weakness full in mind...

Introduction

Welcome to our journey across sun-scorched northern Spain, tracing the French route of the Camino de Santiago de Compostela pilgrimage in pursuit of the headless St. James! This is a tale that interweaves my partner Chris and my experiences hiking the Camino with those of medieval pilgrims. It's a revision of my earlier title, *Blisters and Blessings* and, as you'll discover, there were plenty of each along the way.

What possesses anyone to walk five hundred miles in blistering heat to reach a cathedral housing the supposed relics of a saint? As in the Middle Ages, pilgrims walk for many reasons. We were enticed by my dad, whose description of the swinging silver censer at the Pilgrim Mass in Santiago de Compostela was spellbinding. My parents traveled there by luxury bus, but Chris and I had tested ourselves on other hiking adventures and wanted to know if we were up to this challenge.

In spite of unsightly feet that blister at the mere mention of hiking boots, I have always enjoyed hiking and, in my younger days, tackled England's Pennine Way and, much later, together with Chris, hiked England's Coast to Coast Way, (See my earlier book, *Hiking England's Coast to Coast Way*), the Inca trail to Machu Picchu, and scaled Mt Kilimanjaro.

Chris and I have been much influenced by former British fell walker, Alfred Wainwright, who produced guides to the English Lake District, complete with intricate hand drawn maps. We resonate with his deep love of the outdoors, especially high places, physical exertion, and the thrill of a challenge. Commenting on The Pennine Way, (an approximately 250 mile hike up the spine of Britain), Wainwright said,

"You will find you have enriched yourself, you will be more ready to tackle other big adventures and more able to bring them to a successful conclusion."

He's right, that's why we hiked the Camino (and all the rest). It's my hope that you enjoy reading about our adventures, our joys and our struggles, our Blisters and Blessings, along the pilgrimage route and that you too will be inspired to embrace whatever may challenge you.

If you enjoy *Tracking the Camino de Santiago de Compostela* write a review, follow me on Facebook and Instagram and visit my blog, *Salt Spray and Aspens* at jeangoulden.com

Chapter 1

Sweat sluiced down my spine as we trudged into the northern Spanish town of Najera. It was early afternoon and the temperatures had ignited. There was no shade to be had, we were almost out of water and a little disoriented, struggling to find our accommodation with a map designed to stupefy. When we eventually found the inn, hidden in plain sight, I was embarrassed as I leant over the receptionist's desk, perspiration streamed from my hair, my eyebrows, streaked down my arms and trickled onto the desk. And the scent that steamed from our bodies was feral!

The receptionist seemed unconcerned as, in perfect, barely accented English, she directed us to our rooms. The lift, she apologized, was not working. We had become accustomed to the practice of Spanish lifts taking prolonged siestas so we dragged backpacks, hiking poles, and protesting bodies up the ancient stairs to our refuge. Faded plush wallpaper clad the walls of the dim room and a heat haze hovered over the beds. Instinctively, my partner, Chris, glanced at the air conditioning unit. There was a tinny racket, but no perceptible circulation. Idly wondering if we also had no perceptible circulation, we slumped on the beds. All fastidiousness about allowing our glistening bodies to contaminate the bed coverings had evaporated many hot days ago on the Camino de Santiago de Compostela.

With the resurgence of life force, I sat up and extracted feet from boots, causing a little cloud of dust and debris to mingle with the juicy microclimate of the room. I peeled back my socks and examined my tender feet with caution. They looked like alien appendages, strangely white in contrast to the grime and tan of my legs and arms. Expressing a light sheen of moisture, they recalled the excrescences of an amphibious, perhaps prehistoric, creature. The worst of the throbbing had subsided and it was time to investigate the damage. Tentatively, I slid off the various dressings: there were manageable blisters and the odd bump, but then I examined my right little toe. We were eight days into the Camino by now and the little toe had suffered since day one. It was not a pretty sight. There was a deep-set blister that we had cleaned and drained and dressed before every day's walk. Delicate new skin had formed, but now, it too, bore a bongo blister. Chris, emerging like a swamp man from a primordial shower, peered at it.

"That's not a blister," he said. "That's a wound."

What in heaven's name were we doing? And why? Two questions about which every traveler, every pilgrim, walking this ancient pilgrimage route must shake their dusty heads and wonder.

I blame it all on my dad.

About twenty-five years previously, enticed by a forty percent discount (my dad, after all, is a Yorkshireman of a certain age, one of a dwindling breed, who pride themselves on their thriftiness, claiming that Yorkshire folk are like the penny-pinching Scots but, "with their generosity squeezed out of them"), my parents decided to venture forth, with a throng of other intrepid retirees, on a cruise. So successful was this foray that it launched many other nautical adventures and many renditions of, "For those in peril on the sea," sung in all seriousness on the polished deck of an ocean liner on the Sabbath as the ship cleaved flat, calm waters. Cruising unveiled new panoramas to mom and dad's otherwise modest and sheltered lives.

My dad used to take slides (an archaic concept by now of projecting pictures on a screen) of their ports of call and regale us with stories of their exploits. After many travels, it all became a blur. But the incident that was most vivid, most immediate to me, paradoxically, was the excursion when the camera was left behind. Mom and dad had traveled inland from the port to the city of Santiago de Compostela, in northwest Spain. They had become fascinated by the myths and traditions surrounding St. James (Santiago), the apostle whose bones were said to have been rediscovered near the site of the current cathedral and whose influence had inspired Christian pilgrimage since the Middle Ages (fifth to fifteenth centuries CE).

So great was St. James' appeal that the pilgrimage to Santiago was surpassed only by those to Rome and Jerusalem. At its culmination, lice-ridden, reeking humanity gathered in the great cathedral for the pilgrim mass. It seems unlikely that any of mom and dad's fellow cruise companions were infested and probably reeked only of a cocktail of Chanel No 5 and insect repellent, yet dad relates with awe how a team of vigorous monks swung the giant, billowing censer down the nave of the cathedral.

"You've got to see this Jean," he said, "It's stunning!!"

He was right, I did. But I resolved to walk the pilgrimage route there one day. I'm a journeyer—a seeker after faith and light, the bearer of a dog-eared divinity degree—yet despite my paper qualifications, there have been mutinous moments when I have wondered if there's anything so contrary as religion (at least, the Christian religion with which I am most familiar).

It seems to me that, over time, religious hierarchies spread the expectation that we, the supplicants, should collide a collection of improbable events and interpretations of those events and then step back in reverence and wonder. Even more remarkable is how often this pious paella seems to nourish us. It is a mystery and what a mystery!

The pilgrimage to Santiago, to St. James, is suffused with mystery. I was ineluctably drawn to it and I wondered if its lode was a pull to connect with pilgrims of the past. I had not even a flickering belief that achieving a bunch of bones after much wandering would cleanse me of sin and, in extremes, transport me more rapidly to heaven, as the early pilgrims were encouraged to believe. The ideas of "sin" and "heaven" did not align closely with my views, even though I knew and respected many people for whom this understanding of pilgrimage has deep resonance.

No, I wondered about the pilgrims: Were they a disheveled mob like Chaucer's Canterbury crew, trading insults, bawdy stories, and tales of charity and contrition, or did most travel with fixed and solemn intent? Was their effort, their suffering, their devotion, their faith, their ambivalence, even, as much a part of the landscape as the olive groves, the vineyards, the fields of wheat, and the reverberating bell towers?

If this were true, I had a hunch I wouldn't know it on a rational level, but that I would feel it through the soles of my feet, in my exhausted breath, in my gut. I hazarded this guess since the Camino wasn't my first encounter with that semi-permeable membrane wobbling between the physical and spiritual. I had simultaneously enjoyed and suffered other long-distance hikes and notably climbed the physically and spiritually dizzying Inca Trail to Machu Picchu, Peru. Here in concert with the Camino, the trail traces on the ground the path of the Milky Way above, suggesting an infinite, timeless connection between earthly endeavor and eternal beauty and design. Earlier societies understood the Milky Way as symbolizing a bridge between earth and heaven. The Quechuan, (ordinary) people of the ruling Inca civilization and the medieval pilgrims, navigating by the stars and understanding their governance very differently from most modern folk, would not have underestimated the astral spiritual significance. Both "ways" lead via a sudden turn to a holy place that steals your breath away. Nevertheless, I was still wondering what makes an experience spiritual?

It's a word people lob into the conversation but rarely pause to define. Simply put, I think it is whatever connects us with the divine. But that doesn't necessarily clear things up completely; what do we mean by "divine"? Does this idea help secular folk? Are we talking of a "Higher Power," or something greater than us and our everyday concerns?

Do we just buy into the notion that some places, like the Camino routes, are "spiritual" by their very antiquity? Does a journey, a place, become "spiritual" due to the accumulation of faith, expectations, and hopes of people through the centuries? And do I, together with many of today's "pilgrims," convince myself that the mesmeric trance that prolonged hiking produces is touching our souls? Are there other dimensions, ways of engaging the world that ancient folk intuitively knew and we have all but lost?

So many questions. I suspect that many of us have not lost the desire for spiritual connection, even if it is expressed in contemporary ways.

Celebrated actress Shirley MacLaine hiked the Camino in her sixties and wrote a book about it, The Camino: A Journey of the Spirit, in which she recounts the extended, florid visions she recognized as evidence of previous lives. Believing that the mysterious, elemental power of the Camino route stimulated her visionary experiences, Shirley felt transported back through history to the dawn of civilization, the emergence of gender, sexuality, and creativity.

Although I had no expectation that walking the Camino would impact me as extravagantly as it had Shirley MacLaine, I nonetheless wondered if the mysteries of the pilgrimage could touch me profoundly, provide answers to some of my questions about the confluence of the mundane and the spiritual? I was eager to find out and started by checking my collection of sweaty hiking socks, and unraveling some of the myths and legends of the "way."

· · ● ●· ● ● ● · ·

Jesus commissioned his disciples to spread the good news to the ends of the earth. People believed that James traveled to the Iberian Peninsula, the end of the then known world, close to a place now named "Finisterre" or "end of the land," (a slight overstatement as there is a headland to the south in Portugal that projects farther west).

Quite how James fared in this outpost of the Roman Empire is in doubt. Some suggest that he was feeling downcast when he was visited by a vision of the Virgin Mary. This is Our Lady of the Pillar, who may have been standing on a pillar, or may have presented James with a pillar-like statue of herself that James was to place on the altar of a chapel she instructed him to build.

The town of Muxia recalls the legend in a slightly different fashion. James was at the rugged shore and Mary approached him in a stone boat. The boat was somehow encased in rock and locals suggest that certain parts of the stone boat, such as the sails, can be discerned in the current rock formations. Tradition holds that as well as offering solace, Mary directed James to go back to Jerusalem. His return did not go well. Perhaps, some speculate, due to his irascible nature: his nickname together with his brother John, was, "sons of thunder."

James was beheaded for his faith by Herod Agrippa in 44CE. Apparently, Herod Agrippa wielded the sword personally. Just before his martyrdom, tradition proposes that another aspect of James' character was revealed. Walking to his execution, he healed a man crippled by arthritis.

With the exception of his death, which is recorded in Acts of the Apostles, we have to doubt the authenticity of most of these stories, but they develop a picture of a man worthy of saintly veneration. Passionate, pious, a martyr, and a man moved to compassionate healing in his last, desperate hours. Many a parsimonious pretender has been canonized on far slighter ground. However, this was not the final impression of St. James; the legends surrounding him continued to evolve.

According to the witness of faith, following his death, James was miraculously returned to Spain in a stone boat, or in a stone sarcophagus on board a boat, protected by angels with uncanny navigational skills. One legend suggests that this boat was encased by rock once it grazed the Spanish coast (obviously, this story bears striking resemblance to the detail from the legend of the vision of the Virgin with the Pillar, and suggests the collation of the two stories over time).

James' remains were moved to the site of the current city of Santiago de Compostela. Even this detail of the story is wrapped in legend. Apparently, the seven disciples who had accompanied James' body petitioned the pagan Queen Lupa for assistance. Lupa, feeling that this request offended her own beliefs, determined to frustrate the disciples and destroy James' body by offering the men a team of wild oxen with which to transport James. This colorful story describes how the disciples not only miraculously tame the wild bull oxen, but also defeat a fire-breathing dragon, and culminates with the conversion of Lupa and her offer of a marble tomb in her palace, located approximately at the site of the modern cathedral. Almost eight centuries passed before a hermit, whom we know as Pelayo, rediscovered the tomb, recognizing it as St. James' since two of his less fortunate disciples were buried with the headless body in the marble tomb. Apparently, shining lights and ethereal sounds drew Pelayo to the bones' resting place. Some suggest that this is the origin of "Compostela" or "field of stars." (There is an alternate more prosaic explanation of "compostela" that is a translation of the Latin for burial place.) The local bishop—and later the pope—submitted that these were indeed the apostles' bones.

Veneration of St. James gathered strength and he became associated with further wonders and also was believed to have been the inspiration for the defeat of the Moors.

This shift from preacher to holy warrior began in 944 when James made a miraculous appearance at the Battle of Clarijo (a battle that historians later learned was itself mythic), and persisted three centuries later when James was widely hailed as the Moor Slayer (Matamoros).

In a Spain dominated by Muslims, the figure of the heroic saint depicted as a chivalric knight mounted on a shimmering white horse and trampling Muslims underfoot to reestablish Christendom in Spain, was inspirational to the local Christian people. I always wondered how this image was received by the Moors, the Muslims.

Evidently, I was not alone in my discomfort as there was a movement to remove a statue of St. James depicted on a rampant white steed from the Cathedral of Santiago de Compostela as, not surprisingly, being offensive to Muslims. But tradition won out, and the statue still rears in dramatic overstatement, albeit now cloistered in a side chapel. However, there is an ironic postscript to this part of the tale.

At one time, St. James was venerated in Peru (a land where the Spanish defeated the indigenous population and, so to speak, trampled them and their religious beliefs underfoot). Here, James was seen not as the Moor Slayer, the warrior mascot of the Spanish, or indeed as the slayer of the Inca civilization, but in allegiance with the local people, as Matespanios—Slayer of the Spaniards. The Spanish had brought their precious saint along only to see him turned against them.

In more recent times, this chameleon saint has been understood as a humble pilgrim, bearing the scallop shell that symbolizes the pilgrimage to Santiago de Compostela.

The scallop shell itself attracts legend. It was commonly found on the beaches of Galicia, the region where the pilgrimage ends, and thus was proof that the pilgrims had achieved their goal. Additionally, the grooves on the shell radiating from the base suggest the many routes that converge at Santiago de Compostela, but the prettiest legend refers to James' arrival in Spain as an itinerant preacher. (Another version of this story suggests it occurred when his body was being returned to Spain.) At the time of the boat's arrival, there were wedding festivities. The young bridegroom, happening to notice James' imminent arrival, was powerfully drawn to him and splashed into the sea to accompany him to land. (Sometimes the story claims that he was on horseback or a knight on horseback being drawn under the waves.) As the bridegroom emerged from the waves, he was shining, iridescent with scallop shells. Hence, James was ever after associated with the shell. Nowadays, most modern pilgrims carry a shell across the Camino typically purchased at a souvenir shop, many bearing a sword-shaped cross referencing the belief in James as holy w arrior.

All these changing faces of St. James had the power to intrigue and lure me on over the last eight days, but now here in our clammy hotel in Najera, the only question that intrigued me was, with needle poised, could I bear to prick and drain the blithering blister.

Chapter 2

Rock music pulsed as Chris and I stepped up, onto and down from his sofa. Every time I bobbed up I could see snow falling fast through the apartment window.

"Remind me again why, for the love of God, are we doing this?" Chris asked.

"It's for the headless saint!" I replied.

He shook his own well-tethered head in defeat and started to do lunges. I followed and we lunged alarmingly off-kilter around his tiny apartment, crashing into beds, tables, and, each other. It was what passes for spring in New England and we were preparing to walk the Camino. When I say "Camino" here, it's important to note that there are many Caminos or "ways" to Santiago de Compostela.

In the Middle Ages, people flocked to Santiago from all across Europe. There are routes from Paris and Le Puy, from Portugal and southern Spain, there's the northern route, the primitive route, the via de la Plata or "silver" route, and many others. As we walked the Camino Frances—the most popular modern route, starting on the French side of the Pyrenees at St. Jean Pied de Port—we met people who had started in Germany, Switzerland, and Holland, sometimes walking or cycling from their front doorsteps. There were others, like us, hailing from across the world having traveled by various means to reach one of the acknowledged starting points. Modern Caminos differ in length and in means of transport. There are many who attempt it by bike and a very few on horseback.

After laconic lunges, we lurched into heel raises, side squats, zombie walking steps and, eventually, our arch-nemesis—push-ups. Truth be told, we were a little scared of what we had taken on. Our Camino spans upwards of eight hundred kilometers, (about five hundred miles), we would divide it over three summers, but we would be walking through the hottest season with temperatures likely to be in the high nineties. We had little choice in this; Chris is a teacher and has free time during the summer.

It was well below freezing outside Chris' apartment as we toned and flexed. Since we couldn't walk outside without snowshoes and winter padding, we had decided to follow an online indoor exercise program. And so, we lunged and stepped and pushed-up until we were a quivering blancmange on the floor, tongues drooling for water and the dinner we had heating up in the oven.

As the New England weather relented, we took weekend hikes, sometimes scrambling up the steep slopes of ski runs to build muscle and endurance. We learned that some pilgrims take a dim view of physical preparation, claiming that they would walk themselves fit, or that the medieval pilgrims didn't follow fitness regimes and wasn't this a spiritual journey, anyway?

To be sure, we met some of these people along the way making good progress, covering a farther distance than we did, but they were mostly a good deal younger than us and with more flexibility in their travel plans, allowing them to take a light day or a rest day when they needed it. As for the medieval pilgrims, their situations were vastly different. Those who walked hadn't developed the western sedentary habits of the twenty-first century, the more prosperous folk were on horseback, and most were able to devote as much as a year on pilgrimage.

The idea of a spiritual quest predates Christianity, but by the fourth century CE (well before the rediscovery of St. James' body), Christian pilgrimages were an established expression of piety. The legacy of Roman roads enabled ambitious journeys and the whole enterprise became popular throughout the Middle Ages.

Where Chris and I embarked on the Santiago pilgrimage to challenge ourselves, experience other cultures, and extend our understanding of the spiritual life being expressed through the ordinary, the motivation for medieval pilgrims was quite different. The Christian religion was the predominant and overwhelming influence on the European populace of the Middle Ages, who had little chance of being exposed to other ways of living and believing. Very few could question the church's authority. With the decline of the Roman Empire, the church had based itself in Rome and conducted its affairs in Latin, a language the common folk did not understand and, therefore, could not question.

The church, with its stranglehold on education that was confined in any case to clerics, encouraged the people to believe that their daily thoughts, words, desires, and actions had an impact on the life they would embrace or endure after death. Unexpiated sin would result in a tormented afterlife. To assuage these dismal prospects, the church offered "sinners" various means to avoid eternal damnation, including pilgrimage. Pilgrimages to sacred sites—especially where there were holy relics—could compensate for many a reckless slip. The authenticity of the relic apparently mattered little and Europe was strewn with the ossified body parts of dubious saints and multitudinous fragments of the "true" cross. So, the ostensible motivation for a medieval pilgrimage was to atone for the sins of the past and try to secure a more congenial afterlife. And, this was by no means all!

By taking off on pilgrimage, one could avoid the hounding of creditors who, by law, were not allowed to press their claims. A rich man could employ a poorer to go on pilgrimage on his behalf; all the toils of the journey were endured by the substitute and all the sweets, by the richer man. Modern day pilgrim and author, Ailsa Piper, was so intrigued by this idea that she walked a second Camino, carrying the sins of others for a small fee. She writes about this in her book, *Sinning Across Spain*. It turned out that as she walked, some of her "sinners" began to rethink their past choices or became reconciled to circumstances over which they had no control.

Although many pilgrims were comparatively well-off at the height of the Middle Ages, if a man could find even relatively humble means to support his trip—a trip where hospitality was sometimes freely offered to support the pilgrim's pious intent—he could dispel the monotony of everyday life and venture forth into foreign lands while, at the same time, gaining respect. Women also embarked on pilgrimages, though in far smaller numbers than men, and often in the face of opposition from the church and their husbands. Women were regularly suspected of being "naturally" sinful, lustful, and deceitful, prone to corrupt the endeavors of weak willed men. In 747, St. Boniface petitioned the Archbishop of Canterbury to prohibit female pilgrims traveling to Rome saying, "...a great part of them perish and few keep their virtue, there are very few towns in Lombardy, or France, or Gaul, where there is not a courtesan or harlot of English stock."[1]

· · · ● · ● ● · · ·

And, in the Prologue to the "Wife of Bath's Tale," (a woman who cheerfully exemplified the worst fears of the male dominated community), Chaucer wrote,

> *"Whoever builds his house out of willows*
> *and spur his blind horse over plowed fields*
> *and suffers his wife to go seeking shrines*
> *is worthy to be hanged on a gallows."*[2]

Yet this view did not always prevail; women sometimes went on pilgrimage on behalf of someone else—perhaps a child in grave need. As such they were tolerated, even admired, in their role as caregivers and sustainers. In the miracle stories surrounding shrines, women predominate, petitioning for others or for chronic conditions of their own.

Nonetheless, a pilgrimage was not all delightful, cosmopolitanism. There were dangers to face, storms to weather,

---

1. The Letters of St Boniface trans E. Everton New York Columbia University Pilgrimage in the Middle Ages Studio Gratiana 19 1976, pp. 125-146.

2. Geoffrey Chaucer, The Canterbury Tales; Nine Tales and The General Prologue, ed. V, A. Kolve and Fending Olson, New York, 1989, pp. 120-121.

thieves to outwit, and foreign sickness to survive. Hence, most pilgrims traveled in groups or bands. Regardless of the difficulties, a pilgrimage represented escape, adventure, and an opportunity to experience wonders. Before embarking on a pilgrimage, a pilgrim would present herself to her local priest at a ceremony and often would receive pilgrimage authorization papers. After a blessing and sometimes receiving a penance, the pilgrim would equip him/herself for the journey.

Although Chaucer's pilgrims are described in their everyday dress, from the eleventh century, most pilgrims adopted the pilgrim uniform. Swathed in a long cloak, sheltered by a broad brimmed hat, carrying a soft, scrip or pouch for scant valuables and food, and brandishing a stout staff, the pilgrim would step out on the way.

A few ardent penitents suffered a hair shirt beneath the cloak, a constant reminder of their sinful nature. As well as its practical significance—the cloak served as garment and "sleeping bag"—the uniform not only identified the pilgrim as deserving of succor, but also had a spiritual significance. Apart from serving as a walking stick, the staff was to ward off wolf attacks. There was real danger from wolves in those times, but the wolf also symbolized the devil and hence the staff was a reminder of the spiritual conflict engaged on the journey. The scrip, being small, suggested the pilgrim's poverty and obedience, and the all-encompassing cloak reflected the all-encompassing love of God.

"Help!" Chris texted my children. "Your mother's going to tear the shirt off my back when we reach Santiago!"

That was the plan. For the three summers that we hiked the Camino, Texan Chris had walked every day wearing his faded, torn, off-white "England" t-shirt. True he had rinsed it out most evenings and left it in the room to dry, but it was besmirched with sweat, dust, and a little blood; it hung almost in shreds and was a mosquito magnet.

Chris and I were on opposite sides of the synthetic fiber versus natural fiber debate. He clung to his t-shirt even though it clung to him like bladder wrack, protesting that, in the heat of a Spanish summer, the sweat dried fast and smelled less than the wicking fabric shirts I wore. I was comfortable in these and packed two or three and a long-sleeved shirt that I almost jettisoned several times. We wore hiking shorts and were distinctive in baseball hats. Although ubiquitous in the United States, baseball hats were a rarity on the Camino where a wide range of headgear was sported. My favorites were the trilby and the Chinese coolie hat. We walked in well broken-in hiking boots and clicked up and down the streets with our trekking poles. As a convert to trekking poles, perhaps I overdo my paean of praise. The trekking poles redistribute the weight somewhat, shifting me a little forward and thus avoiding shin splints. They gave me a walking rhythm and added stability when going steeply downhill. As I walk despite low vision, that extra stability is very valuable. Merely carrying the poles prevents the hands from swelling up after prolonged walking and, of course, they were fine prodding sticks for nudging Chris on along the way

Water was by far the heaviest item in our daypacks. We used a Camelback-style hydration system—the kind where water is carried inside the backpack in a heavy-duty bag with a bite-valve on the outside—and supplemented it with water bottles on the most challenging days. The Camino offers many public fountains, but our guidebook advised avoiding these unless you had an iron stomach!

We also packed food for lunch, first aid supplies, suntan lotion, money, and cell phone, that most days seemed utterly irrelevant apart form their camera function. Hardy hikers add a change of clothes and shoes, and a bedroll, but we had opted for an easier trip with extra luggage being sent ahead.

Incongruously, our extra bags contained formal clothes for my family's British weddings and christenings that interwove our Camino, reminding us that this is a journey into life as well as a deliberate detour from it.

Our bags were packed, our bodies strengthened, our hearts were open—even if fluttering a little in anticipation. It was time to leave Boston and head for Spain. At the last moment, Chris threw in a Spanish phrase book... just in case.

· · · · ● · · ● · · · ·

The heat was infernal as we stepped out of the terminal at London's Heathrow airport! Our plans were to change to a regional airport, then fly to Biarritz, France the following day. From there, we'd be picked up by a van for the transfer to St. Jean Pied de Port and the start of our much awaited—and somewhat feared—Camino.

The unanticipated searing temperatures inflamed the hot heads of British drivers as we inched along the melting motorway toward the airport. Our taxi driver, a cheerful cockney when he picked us up, started to fume. He began to curse inflammatorily when he realized we were running out of gas and the sticky traffic jam and spun sugar heat had taken so long that the gas stations had closed. We slid in neutral to the airport hotel past midnight, wondering what other surprises our journey had in store.

Thankfully, if you ignore the fact that the budget airline we flew with to Biarritz made us wear several layers of clothing in order to ensure our lightly packed baggage met their skimpy allowance, the rest of our journey went smoothly and we arrived at the Hotel Central in St. Jean Pied de Port with time to explore this attractive Basque town.

Chapter 3

G eraniums spilled from window boxes, market stalls bustled, and there was a steady procession of unnaturally clean hikers strolling up and down the cobbled rue de la Citadelle, the main street in St. Jean Pied de Port (the "foot" of the "pass"). The attractive town straddles the river Nive in the foothills of the Pyrenees.

Eagerly, Chris and I soaked in the atmosphere, relishing not only the French ambience, but also the more traditional Basque culture of this region of southwest France and northern Spain. We bought round flat Basque bread to go with the French *saucisson* and local cheese we were planning for lunch the next day.

Dinner that evening, eaten on the terrace by the river, featured Basque chicken with a tomato-based sauce and Basque wine. Great cuisine. By this time, we were supplied with scallop shells and soon-to-be discarded floppy hats, and I believed—incorrectly as it turned out—that Chris had photographed everything there was to photograph in this modest town.

Waking early the next morning was not very difficult. We had neither slept well with frissons of excitement and apprehension fluttering through us and melding with the scent of garlic and Gauloises spiraling from the courtyard below our room. Breakfast was a stilted affair. We noted the other early risers, looked them up and down, and feared they were younger and fitter than we were.

After breakfast, with a long, challenging day ahead of us, you'd think we would be on our way. At least, that's what I thought. Not so Chris—he had other ideas. There were more photos to be taken, more nooks and crannies to explore. I felt like a horse, pawing the ground, champing at the bit, ready to spur into action, growing ever more frustrated as I watched other hikers pass us by. It wasn't until much later, after a few more beginnings and endings, that I realized Chris needed to take his time. He needed to make this a ritual, to mark the passage, whereas I needed to get going, to hit my stride and settle into the task ahead. Finally, after a few hurried consultations of the map and after spotting our first Camino sign of the trail, we strode up the hill and out of town.

The Pyrenees are known for their microclimate—often rainy and foggy—and, sure enough, we had not gone too far before we pulled out our waterproofs and began our adventure in a fine rain. Unlike most pilgrims, we chose the Valcarlos option rather than the more impressive route Napoleon. Valcarlos is slightly shorter and less demanding (though it certainly poses its demands if you leave the road and take the steep path out of the valley leading over the abrupt ridge to Roncesvalles—the day's destination for most pilgrims). We would have accepted Napoleon's gauntlet had it not been that our schedule allowed no rest days, we were conscious of being neophytes on this pilgrimage, and our second day promised to take us a little farther than most were planning to walk. We made good progress through pleasant, hilly farmland, walking along minor roads, wondering when we had crossed the border into Spain.

After the first hour, the sun burned through the mist and the rain, and the temperatures built. The road took many dips and lurches, at one time through a small shopping development, and later, in places the path was vastly overgrown, but we pushed through, still a little awed at what we had taken on, yet ready for adventure. By mid to late morning, we climbed steeply up to the first real town, past the first real albergue, (the dormitory-style accommodation that serves the majority of pilgrims), and decided it was time to get our first *sellos*. *Sellos* are rubber stamps hikers collect on their credentials, or pilgrim passports. They're great reminders of where you have been and also serve to prove the pilgrim's entitlement to the certificate to be claimed in Santiago at journey's end.

Strangely we felt self-conscious about this. Would we need to speak French or Spanish, or even Basque? Was it an imposition? We hadn't come this far to wimp out over a detail so, courage in hands, we went into a little store, bought some Werther's Original candy to put a spring in our step, and pulled out the document. In a flash, the storekeeper retrieved her rubber stamp and we were initiated as proper pilgrims. Even though we weren't walking this pilgrimage in repentance or as a spiritual discipline, we came to accept the title "pilgrim," as it was universally and indiscriminately applied.

We felt less than proper as we continued along the road in the firing of a kiln sun. We'd been told there were vultures in these parts so we were keen not to show signs of weakness. We were deceiving ourselves, a passing cyclist stopped to offer water and crackers. She was from New Zealand, having cycled through Germany before embarking on her Camino. It was fun to meet another pilgrim, even the two-wheeled variety; we had walked alone until this point.

Shortly afterward, we passed a field and I wondered if I was hallucinating—it bobbed with plastic dolls' heads—an unnerving crop in their odd-eyed, spiky baldness. They were scarecrows, we realized, not enough to ward off the legendary vultures, but intimidating to lesser birds and disoriented hikers. Before we truly became delusional we thought it was time to take a lunch break.

There was no scenic shady spot, no rustic bench or sylvan glade, but as we turned off the road to join the path that would soon rear out of the valley, we paused at the side of the track, leaning against the slope of the hill. Grimy, sweaty, but very content with our morning's efforts, we tore into the bread and *saucisson*. I swear that food eaten outdoors tastes better than food eaten indoors, and a picnic after strenuous exercise is a feast of delight!

Chris insisted that we drink Gatorade before tackling the next stage—and he was right. The path became so steep that I began to wonder what terrors the route Napoleon held beyond this. In spite of our training, we had to pause to catch our breath, sometimes taking no more than a hundred steps before we needed to take another breathing break. At the precise moment when doubts stormed in as to the folly of this jaunt, we realized the road was in sight. In some ways, this was like a false summit as the path merely crossed the road and continued its precipitous ascent, but before our lungs collapsed we had crested the ridge and were looking down at what was quite literally a breathtaking view—and a signpost that read, "Roncesvalles, 15 minutes."

Can't be, I thought with all the cynical sagacity of one who knows the remarkable elasticity of hiking directions, designed perhaps to demoralize the average walker, who somehow takes a couple of hours longer than the fictitious average walker cited in the instructions. But this time it was true. Within fifteen minutes we were at the pension, ready to kick off our dusty boots.

An hour or so later, with bodies tended, *sellos* stamped, Chris read a leaflet he'd picked up to me since my limited eyesight struggles even with regular- to medium-sized print and this font was tiny. There was a great deal to learn about this area.

"Imagine," Chris said (for he is prone to projections and now was primed with new ideas), "that you are the noble knight Roland. You have been away from home for a long time now on campaign with Charlemagne, your uncle and emperor. It was a worthy cause, to drive out the Moors from Spain and expand Charlemagne's Holy Roman Empire. An empire you believe was preordained by God. However, since you slew the giant Ferragut by spearing him through his navel, little else is going according to plan. You are pulling the militias back, heading toward safer territory. You are weary, longing for home. But you are caught off guard; the enemy launches a sneak attack—you have to join battle once more. The losses on your side are huge—your trusted advisors beg you to retreat, but you have too much pride, and the conflict drags on. The carnage is dreadful; your men are being cut down around you. Finally, you realize that honor cannot be upheld. You reach for Olifant, your hunting horn crafted from the ivory tusk of an elephant. You blow the retreat. You are ashamed you left it so late. So, you blow and blow and blow Olifant, not caring for one more life to be lost needlessly. You use all your stamina to sound the retreat. Your lungs are bursting, your head is hammering. Suddenly, your temples explode. Blood torrents down your body, over your hands and feet. You fall. Death has found you. Its gloating is short-lived. Angels swoop down and bear you up to a glorious, triumphant heaven. Your fame lives on. They write the 'Chanson de Roland' to enshrine you in legend. You did not die in vain."

Squeamish about violence, I nonetheless couldn't help but conjure a gory picture of Roland with his exploding head. I decided that the quiet hiking life and an inconspicuous death would suit me fine, but the story did pique my interest to find out more.

Not entirely unexpectedly, the legend had stretched a few points. The skirmish at the Pass of Roncesvalles took place in 778. Charlemagne's combined forces were in retreat, but they were pursued not by Moors but by Basques. The skirmish was a relatively minor affair except for the fact that a disproportionate number of aristocrats were killed, including the infamous Roland. Over many generations, the oral tradition retold and recast the tale. Somewhere between 1050 and 1115, the "Chanson de Roland" was written, making it the earliest known French poem. The author, or authors, likely were writing in the context of the Crusades and courtly chivalric ideals. Hence the bloodbath at Roncesvalles was romanticized and given epic flourishes; the Moors were demonized probably to bolster the Christians' belief in the justice of their contemporary cause.

From below my window came the sounds of modern day pilgrims gathering for a beer, a meal, and the chance to relive their adventures. I pulled my thoughts away from medieval Christendom and its delusions, from the Crusades, first justified to gain access for pilgrims to the Holy Land, and decided with Chris to gain rapid access to the terrace and the delights of the present evening.

You learn to notice feet. Very quickly. Even if the cyclists have peeled off their spandex and their studs, you know by their posture that they suffer differently from the hikers. Your eyes are drawn inexorably to the flip flops parading nobbles, bruises, corns and blisters. My toes were not a pleasant sight, already sporting tape and Band-Aids. So, our conversation passed from the sublime pleasures of the day's walk through the beautiful mountain passes to the mundane comparison of forlorn feet. It was a juxtaposition to which we would rapidly grow fondly accustomed.

Now it was time to stand on those fragile, yet stalwart, feet and hobble into dinner. Before we did so, we bought a glass of wine each at the bar to toast our success. As we carried the wine into the dining room, we were met with some odd looks. Perhaps we had inadvertently acted as "ugly Americans" (and Brit), and now floundering in a wash of Spanish and Basque culture had acted in a way that was not "de rigueur."

We turned our thoughts to food. (Not a difficult exercise.) The Spanish dine much later than we were accustomed and we had built up healthy appetites. I ordered vegetable soup followed by trout; Chris, bean and pepper soup and duck. The waiter, noticing our struggle to speak Spanish, switched to English.

"What type of wine would you prefer?" he asked.

Thinking that we had offended Spanish sensibilities by bringing in our glasses, we thought we should order another, so Chris ordered red and I white. As the piping, hot hearty soups arrived, so did the wine: a bottle of red and a bottle of white! Now we understood the curious looks! Obviously, we couldn't make much of an impression on that quantity of wine, but we had learned a cultural lesson. In this region of viniculture, dinner is incomplete without an ample sufficiency of wine.

· · • • • • • • · ·

The next morning, we were gathering our things together when we heard a great clattering and stomping outside the room as if a battery of infantry were preparing a campaign.

Chris opened the shutters, leant out of the window and began to film as one hundred and fifty school students and their chaperones lined up, took pictures, and began their Camino. Plenty of others were up and on the move, too.

As soon as we had breakfasted, taken the obligatory photos of each other by the sign that says, "Santiago de Compostela 790," we were ready to go. The distance is measured in kilometers, so seemed especially daunting to those of us who still measure in miles (where it is a mere five hundred).

The only way to reduce the total was to set off, so we stepped out into a lovely morning watching the bright faces of the other hikers on the trail. Perhaps we should have explored more of the cloisters and charms of Roncesvalles, but this was the kind of trade-off we were to make almost every day on the Camino—the lure to linger tempered by the urgent call to carry on.

· · · · ●· ● · ·· ·

The path, at first, was relatively easy leading through verdant countryside and small towns. Although some feel that there are too many pilgrims hiking the Camino in the popular summer months, we enjoyed the company, the diversity, and the sense of belonging. People seemed instinctively to know that they were welcome to talk or to walk on enjoying their own thoughts.

Among the first we met was a group of young men from Slovenia, Germany, and Belgium. Somewhat unimaginatively we nicknamed the latter "Belgian Boy." We'd meet "Belgian Boy" several more times on this section of the Camino. He told us he worked in Belgian television having, together with a friend, pitched their ideas for a show and were invited to produce it. His gregarious nature suggested this was true. We saw him later walking with "Old Dutch Guy," "Tall Dutch Guy," "Danish Girls," and "Korean Dudes," and noticed that his early morning starts got later and later as the week progressed and his night-life developed.

Very soon we came to the town of Burguete—there were signs reminding us that Ernest Hemingway had stayed there in 1924 for a fishing trip he mentions in *The Sun Also Rises*, his acclaimed book set in Pamplona. This captured our attention as we had previously shared an audiobook of Paula McLain's *The Paris Wife*, about his first wife, Hadley. The book centers on their life in Paris and friendship with F. Scott Fitzgerald, Gertrude Stein, James Joyce, Salvador Dali, and other celebrated writers and artists, but we had been most intrigued by their travels to Spain and Hemingway's fascination with the running of the bulls and bull-fighting in Pamplona, just a couple of days away.

We walked briskly through the countryside and small towns, absorbing the enthusiasm of those we met and feeling more confident about this endeavor.

But, the "sun also rises" and it began to beat remorselessly down as the path snaked steeply up. Before long, we had the relief of shade as the trail continued slithering up, but now thankfully, we were between trees and the shade they cast. We marched on until our stomachs clamored hollowly and we found a clearing to tear at yesterday's bread, chorizo, and cheese, watching the other hikers, including "Belgian Boy" and "Old Dutch Guy" stride by, shimmering in sweat.

Just as we'd gained height before lunch, we had to lose it in the afternoon as the path unwound its taut thread toward Zubiri. We wandered a little in Zubiri saying goodbye to fellow hikers, who were mostly staying overnight there. An enterprising taxi driver offered to speed us on to our destination, but we were determined to complete the day on foot despite the glaring sun and the many more hills we faced.

Leaving the town, we crossed the old stone bridge, known as the Rabies Bridge. In days of yore, people used to parade their animals into the water and around its central pier in the belief that this would save them from rabies. It might be apposite to talk of "Mad Dogs and English(wo)men going out in the midday sun" in playwright and composer, Noel Coward's honor, but we were too hot and weary to think, let alone talk or sing.

I was in serious pain from a blister, and Chris had packed his restorative Werther's Original candy in the wrong bag and was craving an injection of sugar to jerk him along the last stretch. Somehow, we dragged ourselves past the bleak industrial site and through the pretty hilltop villages until we reached Hotel Akerreta, where we found hospitality and the opportunity to step into a movie set!

It is not uncommon for those who know we were hiking the Camino de Santiago de Compostela to ask us if we were inspired to do so by the movie, The Way. We had made our plans before seeing the movie starring Martin Sheen whose character walks the Camino in memory of his son who died in an accident while hiking the Pyrenees on the first day of his trail.

It's a journey that gives the father some belated understanding of his son, and transforms his outlook on life. Other characters in the movie learn to be honest with themselves and their superficial motivations for undertaking the trip.

Martin Sheen, whose birth name is Ramon Estevez is a committed Catholic and civil rights activist. He talks of pilgrimage as an internal journey, an encounter with one's true self. Chris saw a discussion of The Way in which it was explained that there are parallels to the *Wizard of Oz*. I was underwhelmed by this, not having made a fundamental connection with the *Wizard of Oz* in my formative years as many Americans of my generation did, but on reflection, I could see that both films are a quest that travels from innocence to experience, from narrow to more open-mindedness.

Arriving at Hotel Akerreta, we recognized the terrace as the setting for some of the scenes in the movie and, as we checked in, our young, friendly host told us that our room was the one occupied by Martin Sheen's character, "Boomer."

We convinced ourselves we recognized it, but when we reviewed *The Way* later, we saw that the camera had hovered there for no more than a second or two. Regardless of any celluloid or digital claim to fame, the hotel was delightful; a converted stone farmhouse built in traditional Pyrenean style with unfolding views of the valley below. Flooding the bathroom after we attempted to rinse out socks and underwear was not so delightful, but was to become one of my signature misfortunes on the Camino!

At dinner, bustling with out-of-town guests as well as residents, we spotted a couple we had seen on our first night in St. Jean. He was tall and balding and she had Asian features. They both appeared to be in excellent physical shape. We walked with them a while the next day and, as they turned out to be Danish, we came up with our first and possibly last inspired nickname, "The Great Danes."

Our hike on the third day was a mere, but enjoyable, fifteen kilometers. We had increased our pace somewhat and had begun to pass other pilgrims. With this new turn of speed and, by dint of taking few breaks, we came level with the "Great Danes" and chatted with them as we walked into Pamplona. They were just sampling the Camino for a week as their family refused to look after their very elderly cat any longer. They asked about our training and were very amused by our descriptions of stepping up on to Chris' sofa and lunging around his apartment. We discovered they were long distance runners, and we felt all the more smug that we had caught up with them. They were headed for a different hotel that evening, so we parted ways and enjoyed *pintxos*, (appetizer-sized delicacies), on the famous square facing the town hall. Other than some exuberant teenagers singing, and incongruously a couple of hikers doing acrobatics even though we had noticed them limping badly as they entered the square, all was calm. Quite unlike the scene here a few days earlier.

Chapter 4

A rocket fired. The tension snapped. Adrenaline-charged runners sprang into their stride and sped down the street. The noise was thunder, an explosion, an earthquake. Bulls blazed down the streets, walls of shining muscle, steam rising from their massive flanks, hooves clanking on the cobbles, blunt heads bulldozing through the melee, a gleam of polished primal horn, a stench of sweat, raw fear, blind, angry, pride. No one breathed, yet everyone was screaming.

Pulverizing power reverberated off the buildings, through the lungs and hammering hearts. The riptide of bulls swept down the streets. Runners panicked, scrambled over barriers, fell, and brought each other down. Smears of white and red on the road, broken bodies. The rocket released the chaos monster and here was the minotaur, the aurochs shattering the dark cave and torpedoing towards the ring. The runners careered into the amphitheater. Alive with thrill, relief, comradeship and the clamoring question, "Can we quell the beast?"

Much later, when the blood moon had risen, an elderly priest, with scarred face and shrunken body murmured, "Which beast? The one who dwells within?"

At the closing ceremonies of the San Fermin, all the bulls, and some of the humans lay dead.

At first, Chris was more attracted to Pamplona's San Fermin fiesta with its encierro (running of the bulls) and bullfights than I was, half wishing we had arrived a few days earlier to witness the spectacle. I was repulsed by the horror and brutality of it all and had to take some time to process these gory festivities.

Technically, the festival is in honor of Saint Fermin, the patron saint of the region of Navarre and of its historic capital city,

Pamplona. Not much is known about Fermin other than that he lived in Roman times, professed Christianity, and shared St. James' fate of quite literally losing his head. Apparently, on his death, a beautiful scent emanated from his remains that had healing powers. At the start of the *encierro*, the runners pray for San Fermin's protection—as one experienced runner explained—for a few seconds, even the most ardent atheist is willing to believe in the power of prayer.

The festival takes place with exuberant celebration from July sixth to fourteenth.

Afterwards, the town soon gets over its exhaustion and maintains a countdown clock to remind the townsfolk of how long they need to wait before the next San Fermin madness is unleashed. Quite when the celebration of a healing saint melded with bull-fighting traditions is unknown, though there are written records of the encierro dating to the Middle Ages. I wonder what an unsuspecting pilgrim of those times made of it all. Did it strike them as barbaric or exhilarating? Did they live more closely with this kind of violence than we do, truly sourcing their food locally and finding entertainment in animal baiting? Did they find some spiritual significance in it all, or was it merely a welcome diversion for weary wanderers?

On reflection, it seems to me that the festival accesses something profoundly primitive in us, in the same way that some myths touch us; we barely understand, but we are moved anyway. Joseph Campbell, the renowned expert on world mythology reminds us of the prevalence of the "great animal" myths of hunting societies. The great animal laid down its life for the community, was venerated and respected. The great animal was the food source for a community and therefore supplied the life force. The people took their strength from one who was stronger than they. The meat from the Pamplona bulls is also subsequently eaten; however, the argument that these are necessary dramatic deaths is easily refuted. Bulls' sacrifice has distant roots, dating at least since biblical times and the Canaan god Baal was depicted as a bull. The bullfight is a ritual killing and I'm sure its proponents would declare it is highly respectful of the bulls. The fiesta still shocks me, but I understand that it pulses on a level that makes us question if the animal and spiritual natures of living creatures are deeply intertwined.

Not having to confront the festival head on, we enjoyed our stay in Pamplona; we had arrived early enough to make it feel like a rest day. After siesta, when the shops and public buildings really do close, we strolled through the streets replenishing our supplies of Werther's and buying an odd array of items—iodine, a watch-strap, needle and thread, a ponytail scrunchie, and some toothpicks, all negotiated via sign language or the merest smattering of Spanish.

Chapter 5

W e left Pamplona early the following morning in an attempt to cover as many miles as possible before the heat of the day. From now on we would even sacrifice breakfast, something Chris swore he would never do, to this end. Since I have low vision and can't walk in the dark, there were always hikers who had risen before us striding out in the distance.

Once we left the Pamplona suburbs, we were again in beautiful countryside, dotted with sleepy hilltop villages built of warm stone. Even though we had enjoyed our time in Pamplona, it felt as if we were getting back to the "real Camino." Of course, this was an arrogant thought; we only had three days' experience of the Camino, ywr they were days that had fully absorbed us. We had left our everyday cares and worries far behind and already identified closely with the other hikers we met along the way.

In time, the path began to rise steeply and I realized we must be climbing the hill that is fringed with the famous pilgrim monument. Most find the climb challenging, but the view from the top is spectacular. The pilgrim monument sculpted by Vincent Galbete in 1996 depicts a procession of pilgrims through the ages, some on horseback, headed toward Santiago de Compostela. Strangely, despite the poetic dedication, "Where the wind crosses with the stars," I found this monument less compelling than most. As I said, I had already identified with modern day pilgrims, but the feeling that I was walking in the steps of history took longer to inhabit me.

You miss a lot walking the Camino. There is only so much you can absorb, and since my vision problem makes reading a guidebook very difficult, I missed two significant things about this climb. First, we were completely oblivious to the Fuente de

La Renierga. This is a fountain and the site of one of the most notorious legends of the Camino.

Wreathed in the mists of time, a depleted pilgrim staggered to this spot, suffering from exhaustion and dehydration. Recall that a medieval pilgrim could not have availed himself of a flight to Biarritz and a van to St. Jean Pied de Port—at this point, he could have traveled for many months, faced all kinds of dangers, and might well be in woeful condition. The devil pounces on the opportunity and offers the bedraggled pilgrim water if he will renounce God. The pilgrim declines. The devil persists, promising the tantalizing water if the pilgrim will renounce the virgin, but the pilgrim resists once more.

Again, the devil tempts the pilgrim. "Renounce your faith in Santiago!" With an effort of will, the pilgrim once more resists. And then of course, he is rewarded as an indomitable apostle appears, who cowers the quailing devil into quenching the pilgrim's thirst before he faints. Close by, there is a church, where remains of pilgrims complete with scallop shells were found. Given the exigencies of the journey and the fact that some walked in hope of healing, it was inevitable that pilgrims would perish on their journey. (A journey of at least twice the modern distance as most would also have had no choice but to walk back home.)

It probably took years before their friends and family realized some would not return. Unless they were in deep disguise, we encountered no apostles, devils, or expiring pilgrims. We *did* meet another Danish woman, the Danes being the most populous of our companions to date. She was taking a break, by the monument, to rest her knee with its torn meniscus. We found that she had walked with her boyfriend all the way from Geneva. She was the first of our fellow walkers to get to the heart of the matter, volunteering that she was walking because there were some things she needed to leave behind.

We instantly liked her for her courage, candor, and strength, but as there was no sign of a boyfriend at the time, we worried if he was one of those things that had had to be left behind.

I had also missed that the hill is named "Alto de Perdon." This means "Peak of Forgiveness." It takes its name from a nearby thirteenth century church, where the virgin was said to ensure the forgiveness of sins and safe passage to Santiago.

We scrambled down the sheer descent from Alto de Perdon and pressed on into the region of Navarre with its artistically arthritic olive trees and trellised vineyards. The scenery was beautiful, but the temperatures had soared once again and we could find no shelter for lunch. In the end, we settled for a scraggly bush by the roadside that gave us the illusion, but not the reality, of a shaded place. In spite of the good salami and local bread, we didn't rest for long, hoping to reach Puente la Reina, and the comparative cool of its hostel, before we dissolved drip by drip into the rich red earth of the region.

We arrived in Puente la Reina (named for its famous bridge, built in the eleventh century at the behest of Queen Dona Mayor (La Reine) for the convenience of pilgrims), our bodies glossy with sweat, early in the afternoon as the locals were heading off for siesta. We retrieved our bags that had arrived in the hostel basement hours earlier.

Despite the cobwebs and the musty smell, it was cool down there and we were tempted to linger. Instead, we lugged the bags upstairs (the lift being petulant at that time of day), and embarked on our routines of resting, cleaning, foot inspection, laundry, reading and note taking.

When we emerged a couple of hours or so later, the day was humid as well as hot, but our spirits cheered as we saw some of our Camino friends arriving. The Camino is an unwinding of the road and of life, not a race, so we swallowed our inclination to tease them about how slowly they had walked. When they sprawled at the trestle tables and ordered beer, I had to move one of their backpacks. I was glad I hadn't chided them; the packs were stone heavy, since unlike us they weren't having their luggage sent on ahead.

We joked and chatted for a while until Francois jerked his head up from the guide book, "Mon dieu!" he exclaimed. "They hung my countryman, Jacques de Troya, here back in the fourteenth century."

It turned out that Jacques had been pilfering the other pilgrims' provisions and he had to pay a ghastly price.

The supermarket in town extracted only a reasonable amount of euros and no terminal fees when we restocked our supplies. We took an advance look at the famous bridge we were to cross the following day before climbing steeply out of town and wending our way through more attractive hill villages that looked likely to furnish early risers croissants and coffee au lait.

Chapter 6

"... I'll tell you what I want, what I really, really want
So tell me what you want, what you really, really want
I'll tell you what I want, what I really, really want ...."

No, it wasn't the Spice Girls walking just ahead of us, performing their hit song, but three more dazzling Danish girls singing as they strode through the vineyards. We were sandwiched between them and the whole procession of Spanish students we had seen leaving Roncesvalles. They were in good humor, too, singing first something in Spanish and then striking up "Doe a deer, a female deer." The Danish "Spice Girls" were a tough, entitled act, but soon they were overcome by "The Sound of Music" and joined in.

We sang as we walked for several kilometers and, motivated by the singing, Chris and I pulled ahead. A couple of towns later, we found a delicious shady spot by a river for lunch; however, we didn't have the place to ourselves—it was thickly populated by young couples in deep clinch. Having felt young, vigorous, and happy during the morning, we now felt old and self-conscious. Nonetheless, we enjoyed our lunch washed down with copious quantities of by now tepid water. Given the heat and the exertion, it was necessary to keep well hydrated, but I began to regret it an hour or so later when my bladder became insistent on relief.

We had reconnected with many other pilgrims and were again walking through the farmland while being slowly rotisseried by the early afternoon sun. There was almost no shade, so obviously no large bushes, rocks, trees or any natural phenomena to provide a screen for personal matters. My bladder was calling the alarm now and I walked on in increasing discomfort and distress.

Finally, I came upon a tufted tumulus in a plowed field, part protected by a thin hedge. There was barely enough cover, but it would have to suffice. Fearful of discovery, I rushed the operation, hastily rearranging underwear and hiking shorts. I rejoined Chris, who was highly entertained by the whole episode.

"What are you doing now?" he asked, as I kept itching my derriere.

"Never you mind," I replied, realizing that the field and now my nether garments were full of thistles, briars, and sticky-buds. Many launderings later, they laid in ambush for me. Scratchily, in my case, we regained our companions, walking now with the Dutch, Canadians, and the Koreans with whom we had no mutual language, so they bowed and we smiled and high-fived in response.

Despite the heat, badly blistered feet, rasping underwear, and rivulets of salty sweat splashing like whitewater off my brow, my arms, my spine, it was fun walking into Estella in the company of others who seemed to share the belief that this was a meritorious rather than foolhardy adventure. Just as we turned into town, we saw the school party, who must have indulged a shorter lunch break than we had. They were lounging near the banks of a river, but two or three were lying palely in the shadow of a tree, being fanned by the organizers and watched over anxiously by friends. I guessed they had heat exhaustion and felt that my vast water intake had been worthwhile in spite of the embarrassing and unintended consequences.

We hailed the King in Estella as he passed by on his white horse accompanied by sackbut and drum. The royal steed appeared indifferent to the medieval blanket it bore in addition to the sovereign, but his attendants, in tunic and clinging hose, looked piglet pink but not perky.

It was Medieval Festival week in Estella, highly appropriate for this town that flourished in the Middle Ages. Although communities had gathered in earlier times, the town owes its expansion and historic importance to King Sancho Ramerez who, in the eleventh century, decided to attract foreign merchants from France and Germany to settle in the town and to offer hospitality to the growing number of pilgrims on the Camino de Santiago de Compostela. Town charters were granted in 1066 and again in 1164. The 1164 charter has specific provisions to prevent the abuse of pilgrims. The town, from time to time, earned the appellation, "Elegant Estella," and there are many wonderful medieval churches, palaces, civil buildings, and gracious squares.

Our hotel, newly refurbished and particularly comfortable, nestled in the lee of the great church Iglesia de San Miguel Arcangel rising dramatically from a rocky outcrop. We emerged refreshed from its comforts to explore the hot town and replenish our provisions. Like other Spanish cities in this region, its streets were narrow and its buildings quite tall so that they would cast protective shadows on the merchants, pilgrims, and townsfolk.

Today, many of the townsfolk were clad in medieval garb and there were several pleasant distractions. We strayed across the medieval market admiring first the leather products that the town's erstwhile tanneries would have manufactured, and then lingering at the medicinal stall. Here was every kind of root, herb, and elixir to promote healing and well-being.

I remembered from childhood history lessons that, in medieval times, ill-health was thought to stem from two causes: interference by the devil, or the imbalance of various humors; different colored bile, blood and phlegm. The remedies were applied to correct the imbalance. To some extent, Arabic medicine had proceeded on more scientific principles and I was curious to see if pilgrims would have encountered Islamic remedies in Moorish Spain.

It seems that this is a complicated question as the Middle Ages encompassed a huge sweep of time and the extent to which new medical practices were integrated would vary from place to place according to communications, the local populace, and the influence of individual physicians.

Undoubtedly, by the fourteenth century, Islamic medical knowledge had spread to the West as Chaucer describes the doctor who traveled with the Canterbury pilgrims:

"With us ther was a DOCTOUR OF PHISYK...
For he was grounded in astronomy...

He knew the cause of everich maladye,
Were it of hoot or cold, or moiste, or drye,
And where engendred, and of what humour...
Wel knew he the olde Esculapius,
And Deiscorides, and eek Rufus,
Old Ypocras, Haly, and Galien;
Serapion, Razis, and Avicen;
Averrois, Damascien, and Constantyn;
Bernard, and Gatesden, and Gilbertyn.[1]

As well as knowing astronomy, natural magic and the humors, this doctor was well-versed in the work of famous Greek, Islamic, and European physicians. Whatever treatment the pilgrims received they would have received it in a hospital. This term had a slightly different meaning compared with its modern usage. Hospitals were places of hospitality for the needy; this could mean blind people, orphans, people unable to work, travelers, or pilgrims, and they would receive shelter and such care for their needs as could be provided. As some pilgrims undertook pilgrimage in the hope that the influence of the apostle's bones would cure their ailments, some were ill before they undertook the travails of the journey. Often, these "hospitals" evolved into modern day inns or hotels, and indeed it was in one such *hospederia* we were spending our night in Estella.

For our well-being, we were relying, perhaps slavishly, on modern science, and were carrying pain killers, anti-inflammatories, anti-diarrheal medicine, even some antibiotics, along with Band-Aids, knee supports, and blister remedies. I wondered, for a brief moment, if a gentle infusion, a poultice, or a salve would have caused us to slow down, rest, reflect and soothe our bodies and souls. But I left it at wondering; I wasn't eager to try many of the more outlandish concoctions on offer at the market.

---

1. Geoffrey Chaucer, The Canterbury Tales; Nine Tales and The General Prologue, ed. V, A. Kolve and Fending Olson, New York, 1989, pp. 120-121.

Regardless of medical intervention, most medieval pilgrims would understand "dis-ease" as evidence of evil arising from sin and satanic temptation that could only be overcome through divine favor. God could perhaps be wheedled into miraculous intervention through prayer, through visiting the reliquaries of saintly body parts that littered Europe, or through pilgrimage. Disease, of course, was a serious issue in medieval times; the population was decimated by plagues in 1348, 1362, 1380, 1400, and 1420.

It's easy to shrug off such epidemics believing that they belong to a bygone age, yet modern day "plagues" still ravage populations in the developing world and among disadvantaged people across the globe. As climates change, new or different viruses and bacteria pose new threats, as we learned during the worst of the Covid years.

We moved on, back toward our hotel, desirous of one of the modern era's most sanitizing offerings—beer! We settled ourselves in a "food tent" and bar erected between our hotel and the edifice of the towering church. It was unclear if this tent was solely for the festival or whether it served a wider market. Its menu was very restricted, offering octopus cooked in copper pots, or ribs for the faint of heart. We learned that octopus is a Galician specialty, and also a favorite at festivals. But now we quaffed a beer, far safer for the pilgrims of the past and the local populace than was the untreated water. As the website aromasysabores.com reminds us, the polluted water could occasionally kill a horse!

The Great Danes slipped in along the benches across from us; they too, were enamored by this lovely and interesting town, but also in compelling need of a refreshing beer.

Our hotel did not provide dinner that night, but instead the receptionist directed us to a local restaurant across the old Jewish quarter of town. I had known that Muslims had taken over much of Spain and that the Christians had thought of them as the infidels, and had defeated them or caused them to convert to Christianity in the late fifteenth century, but it had not occurred to me that there had been Jews in these parts since pre-Roman times.

Apparently, biblical references to Jewish presence in Tarshish may have indicated modern Spain. By the thirteenth century, one percent of the population of Estella were Jews, some holding high civic office. Unusually, there was a separate synagogue for women. But in 1328, during Navarre's civil war, much of the Jewish population was wiped out.

Later, five men were accused of perpetrating the crime. Their hands were cut off and they were hanged for the offense. It was not until 1498 that Navarre expelled the Jews, those who remained at that time generally converted to Christianity.

When we reached the restaurant, unpromisingly located in a back alley, we were greeted by some familiar faces, the three Danish "Spice Girls" of earlier in the day, Belgian boy and his companions, the bowing Korean, the Great Danes, and a couple from Australia who originated in Brazil and Britain. There appeared to be no Spaniards, not necessarily a bad sign as at 8:00p.m., it was still early by their standards.

As we found our table we heard strains of a medieval procession in the distance. Quickly it was upon us with drums and pipes and cheerful yet raucous shouts. Many of the revelers were encased in outlandish contraptions of streamer-strewn monsters and several supported a wiggling water snake with hinged mechanical, wooden jaws. He snapped at my napkin as he passed, but we were without camera to snap back.

We ate the regional specialties, braised pork for Chris and mouth-watering rabbit for me. As we were investigating the local dessert, a man approached our table. He was tanned and muscular and his glossy blue-black hair was swept back into a sleek ponytail.

He talked ardently for some time, but we only understood one word, "Trotsky." Quite why he had singled us out, or what he needed to impress upon us, we never worked out. Maybe he was a Basque separatist and seeing that our spoons were poised over the Basque dessert had wanted to enlist our sympathy. People in this region of Spain eat a lot of milk-based desserts, translated as "junket" in our phrase book. I tasted mine in happy anticipation. It was repulsive–having a dominant flavor of acrid wood ash!

Seeing my reaction, Chris liberally added honey, and filmed himself using his phone as he attempted to swallow the dessert. We were laughing at his performance as we heard the procession approach again. This time, we captured it on the phone complete with water serpent lunging for the delectable dairy dessert!

Eventually, we left the colorful restaurant and repaired to our designer "hospital." The town partied all night, apparently not unusual on a summer weekend, but we slept soundly irrespective of the threat of strangulation by the washing line Chris had stretched across the room. We were very content, and for once I hadn't flooded the bathroom.

Chapter 7

We high-fived the bowing Korean man before we climbed the steps of the attractive medieval bridge leaving Estella. It was early Sunday morning, and although we were sad to leave Estella, Chris was a man with a mission. Whereas you might expect to find a mission in a monastery, we were to pass by the Monastery d'Irache with barely a backward glance.

We were in search of a significant fountain—the one that flowed with wine. It was still well before nine when we reached the Bodegas Irache—a winery that offered free wine to pilgrims. Almost everyone stopped here and even at this hour of the morning we had to wait while two cyclists and an Italian hiker refreshed their spirits. I poured a little wine onto my scallop shell in traditional pilgrim fashion, and then I learned that there is an art to drinking from shells—sticky little trails of red wine slithered down my arm and mingled with the morning's secretions. We neither drank enough even on an empty stomach to approach intoxication, but we smiled and clinked tippy scallop shells as Chris read the translation of the sign above the fountain.

"Pilgrim, if you wish to arrive at Santiago full of strength and vitality, have a drink of this great wine, and raise a toast to happiness."

We definitely felt cheered by our Sunday morning's baptism in wine and encouraged to press on through the beautiful countryside to Los Arcos. The hiking was relatively easy on gravel paths through fertile agricultural land and we reached Los Arcos by lunchtime where we rejoined the Brazilian-British-Australians.

To my amazement, they confessed (this was Sunday after all) that they had no blisters. My feet had screamed at me since

Roncesvalles and even Chris, who generally has hardy feet, was tending to a couple of clamoring blisters.

Los Arcos is dominated by a huge and lovely church and by many clock towers and bells. They sounded every quarter as we noted throughout the night. My expectation had been to rest up here and reflect on the spiritual revelations of the Camino—after all, as I noted, it was the Sabbath.

We lounged on a balcony overlooking a town square and wiggled our bare pale battered toes in this open-air sauna, but it was too hard to meditate, to reflect. This little town, important once for straddling the crossroads of Navarre and Castille, was today a crossroads for bikers, buses and heavy agricultural vehicles—there was no peace even when the locals slipped inside for their siestas. I read my book—a humorous memoir—and thought how grateful I was for my strength and vitality, the company we kept, and Chris' ever cheerful companionship.

· · · ●·● · · ·

Dawn was barely cracking a chink as we left Los Arcos the following day. We had scouted the paths and they were gravel and straight for a few kilometers so that even with my low vision we could make some early progress on what promised to be a long and challenging day. We were headed thirty kilometers to Logrono and what felt in a way like a new start. At dinner the previous evening, we had discovered that several of our new-found friends were only walking the first week on the Camino and were headed home today.

We questioned, "How would the great nation of Denmark be represented in the weeks to come?"

We hit our stride and covered a great deal of distance before the sun rose and started to toast the countryside, the towns, and the footsore pilgrims. As we constantly walked toward the west, we were developing very lopsided tans. I imagined what I would look like at the family wedding we were attending in a couple of weeks' time with one brown arm and one white one! It wasn't important—that's one of the things you learn on the Camino—stick to essentials and let go of the rest. We both felt we had let go of the need for coffee for too long as we approached Viana.

As we lurched, hobbled, shuffled, or strode into these summer Spanish towns, it often felt as if they were celebrating our limp arrival, and so it was with Viana. Music was playing, bunting strung across the streets and young visions in white and red were running around in high spirits. Firecrackers spluttered in excitement. Glad as the Spaniards were for the income pilgrims brought to a country recovering from recession, the festivities were not actually in our honor!

We had stumbled upon festival week complete with bull running and fighting. Energy rang from the stone walls and passageways and we feared the town was too full to supply us with coffee and croissants, or somewhere to sit in the shade and drink in the atmosphere. But we found a place down an alley alongside the church famous for being the site of Cesare Borgia's burials!

We stripped off the backpacks and I elevated my feet even though that provoked increased throbbing. As I did so, I knocked our hiking poles onto the table adjoining ours. I apologized to the couple sitting there and wondered what reception I would get for disturbing their morning musings. They were an elegantly dressed older couple, definitely not hikers, and I questioned how they felt about the invasion of their town and their privacy.

My concerns were misplaced—they were delightful, and soon we were swapping life stories. Chris emerged bearing the coffees to learn that the husband had been born in Afghanistan, raised in Persia and British Aden. Although they lived abroad now, his wife had once been a Viana girl and they returned each year for family reunions and the festival.

Our stories of a Yorkshire lass and a Texan lad seemed tame in comparison, but they welcomed us warmly and offered to help should our fortunes flounder. They also told us more about the life of Cesare Borgia of whom we only had fleeting recollections. It turns out he was born the illegitimate son of Pope Alexander VI, in the late fifteenth century. By the time he was twenty, his father had appointed him as a cardinal, but he fancied himself as a man of action rather than a man of the cloth and resigned the cardinalate. He spent his manipulative, deceitful, brief life in pursuit of power and is said to be the model for Machiavelli's *The Prince*. His ambitions might have been realized had his father not succumbed to malaria. Cesare himself contracted the illness and survived it *and* the cure—immersion in a vat of ice water.

With the advent of the new pope, he was sent to Spain and imprisoned, but he managed to escape and returned to Navarre to support his brother-in-law, King John of Navarre in the siege of Viana. Through his own misjudgment, he was killed in a skirmish outside the town. King John built a marble mausoleum for Cesare's remains that were laid near the altar in the church of Santa Maria in Viana, but he was not allowed to rest in peace for long. Following political and ecclesiastical changes, his remains were exhumed and cast beneath the street. Over the centuries, they were dug up and reburied several times and were kept in the Town Hall for several decades. Eventually, in 2007, they were returned to the church, perhaps his final resting place.

Reluctantly, we left our friends, their good stories, and their warm wishes and walked from the comfortable shade of the café into the blistering square and on, out of town into the countryside of Rioja, verdant with vines and olive trees and splashed with wild flowers. Shortly after lunch, we found the red tarmac road that leads to Logrono. It is red to reflect the wine of the region, but it offers no mercy from the sun for some distance. Then we spotted a woman seated at a souvenir table under the shade of a tree and hurried to this oasis.

She sold us cool drinks, a new scallop shell for me (I had lost mine sometime after the wine fountain), and offered us *sellos* for our credentials. Later, we were told her prices were exorbitant, but we didn't care—it was a luxury to share the shadow of the tree with her.

Somewhat refreshed, we walked the last rather tedious miles into Logrono and with the aid of three maps, found our hotel and the glory of a shower! Logrono is a large town, neither ugly nor particularly attractive, and we were staying in a large modern hotel catering to the business community. Despite its air-conditioned amenities, we missed the camaraderie of the smaller inns, the multi-lingual narrative of the shared journey.

Our fondest memories of Logrono were in the early evening, when we escaped the hermetically-sealed rooms, the air-freshened, well-functioning elevators, the impersonal foyer, and went in pursuit of duct tape, sunscreen, and Werther's! We achieved all three after much sign language, rough sketches, consultations with the phrase book, and a liberal dose of hilarity. The people were all anxious to help, drew us fairly accurate maps of where to go, and claimed us as dear amigos! The contrast between the sterility of the hotel and the warm embrace of the local people was not lost on us.

Early the next day, we stepped out of the artificial chill of the reception area and into an already hot and surprisingly humid morning. By the time we reached Navarette, two or three hours later, the humidity had cleared, but we were sticky, hot and bothered, and disappointed that the guide book's promise of a plethora of cafes and bars was a gross exaggeration.

We sat on a lopsided bench and munched wilting muesli bars and a dry roll left over from our hasty, sparse breakfast. As usual, we walked amidst wonderful scenery; vines, cherries, and olives flourish in the rich, wine red earth. But today we hardly noticed the natural beauty, the valleys opening up beneath our feet. The sun was baking us into the ground, melting us into the tarmac and fricasseeing us into the fields. We paused in the shade of a bridge as the path ran along the main road for a while. There was Spanish graffiti and a dubious smell, but it was the coolest place around for a number of miles, so we lingered there.

Before long, a small crowd of parched pilgrims had gathered too. We panted and nodded but no one had the energy to converse until the Germans arrived. There were four of them in great spirits, joking that our water systems must surely contain beer! Buoyed by their enthusiasm, we followed them out on to the Camino again and lurched a few more killing kilometers to a hillside café. Having achieved ice-cold Cokes, we were recovering when we heard German guffaws from the terrace outside.

The Germans had found their beer and were fueled to hike into Najera. Reluctantly, we left the café and marched out into the unrelenting blast furnace. We again appropriated Noel Coward's genius and made up a silly song, based on his hit, "Mad Dogs and

Englishmen go out in the midday sun" adapting it to, "Mad Tex and English chicks go out in the midday sun." We chanted it over and over to distract ourselves from the endless hot drudgery of the walk.

Finally, envious of the long loping strides of the Danish woman we had met at the Pilgrim monument several days ago, and who now overtook us with grace and ease, we made it to a little stream. There was just the illusion of a breeze here, so we paused for a few minutes as Chris read the many twenty-four-hour taxi signs nailed to the tree! Clearly, we were not the first to be approaching Najera in a condition close to collapse. I think it took Chris an effort of will not to dial for help, but we were on the outskirts of town—civilization and most importantly, a shower, were within our grasp.

Hours later, the two people who emerged from that humid hotel room in Najera were transformed. It was as if every cell in our bodies had inflated as we cooled down, drank more water, rinsed away the sweat, washed our bedraggled hair and reset our expectations for the following day. In spite of the now pierced, drained, and tended blister, I had a spring in my step as we walked along the riverbank to a café where the "Jolly Germans" as we now thought of the foursome, were enjoying a large stein of beer!

After a day of struggle, we were now lighthearted, relaxed, on vacation, because our transformation had been emotional as well as physical. Even though the next day's hike was relatively short, we had decided to treat ourselves to a rest day and take the bus! In a sense this was a defeat; we were on a pilgrimage, we were walking to Santiago de Compostela tracing the footsteps of the medieval pilgrims, we were challenging ourselves, finding out if we could gain spiritual insights through the physical impact of walking for many days. On the other hand, this was no defeat but a return of sanity! Surely medieval pilgrims hitched a wagon ride once in a while!

My determination to get to Najera had been all consuming to the extent that I had not realized that we weren't enjoying ourselves anymore. Now, with the prospect of a day's rest, we were already refreshed and ready to embrace whatever this rather lovely town sheltered by tall, rocky cliffs, had to offer.

Mercedes and Victor—they were the town's offering to us! We were enjoying a leisurely Spanish dinner in the back-alley restaurant that our hotel had recommended when a little girl skipped toward us. She was about four years old and her eyes glowed with curiosity and mischief! She was totally unflustered when she learned that we spoke English and demonstrated her facility in counting in English. *One, two, three, seven, ten.* Then she pointed at the bread and asked us the English name. Next, she pointed at herself and proudly told us she was Mercedes. Our names underwhelmed her entirely!

As the evening drew on, Mercedes brought members of her family to meet us and then ran off to play with her little brother, Victor. A number of adults had been idly supervising the children, but the last shift was down to dad. Sorry, dad, but Mercedes wound you round her cocky, little finger and even got Victor into trouble for one of her own misdemeanors. We were entranced, and eventually wandered back to our room treasuring some very happy memories of our time in Najera!

Chapter 8

N ext day, the bus ride to Santo Domingo actually seemed miraculous. The scenery flashed by so quickly and we were astonished how soon we arrived. It's not as though we live isolated from modern transport—it's simply a symptom of how deeply enmeshed we had become in our pilgrimage. We had a lovely tourist day in Santo Domingo de la Calzada, stopping first by a bakery where we bought "dead boy bread" and gleaned something about one of the town's sustaining myths.

We toured the cathedral making sure to include the ecclesiastical chicken coop we had learned was associated with the myth. Then we checked into our *hospederia* which was run by nuns who, in full habit, after vespers, served us dinner with the inevitable and obligatory bottle of wine. At lunch, we lingered at a café in the plaza and befriended the waitress who was so kind as to imitate a pig in order to translate the menu for us! She was very accommodating and surprised to find Americans willing to linger and stutter in Spanish. She shared with us some of the stories of Saint Domingo, the founder of this interesting town. I was intrigued and inspired by the rich weave of this town's hiaroey so, during siesta, I indulged in a little whimsy and wrote some playful postcards from Santo Domingo de la Calzada.

· · · ● ● ● ● ● · · ·

From Gregorio to the faithful at Osteja:

Ridding the land of locusts is wearisome work and thus it was that I took to strolling in the forest near Ayuela.

I chanced upon a humble hermit by the name of Domingo Garcia. My spirits lifted as I conversed with this most worthy man. Disappointed in his desire to join the Benedictine brothers being no scholar, he had retired to the forest and, noting the perils encountered by the pilgrims wending their way to the shrine of St James, he determined to aid their passage. No longer are they obliged to ford the river, for Domingo will build them a sturdy bridge and a good paved road. No longer must they rest their weary bones amid the mold and must of the forest floor, for Domingo has in mind to build them a hospital. My soul warmed and I knew him for a holy man, so I ordained him priest, and gave him land for his establishments.

I am not customarily given to flights of fancy, but it would not be too great a wonder if Domingo should hence become a saint, Santo, and have a town named in honor of his gracious hospitality.

· · · ● · ● · ● · ·

From Hester, the harassed hen, to the fowl of the land:

Such a fine mess there is here as ever I knew. That pea-brained rooster keeps strutting around this holy hen-house as if he built the creaking cathedral. He crows night and day as if he'd never heard of dawn! My head rings so, I'm in a right flap. And then the bell chimes and the organ moans, I'm tempted to tweak the parson's nose! The kindly keeper tells me it's not long before I can prance back to the farmyard and scratch in the dust, and some other broody birds will have to suffer a month cooped up in here. And the people who come to gawp at us—I never saw such tousled sorts. Anyone would think they'd walked across Spain to take a peek at us. What do they expect? They've stuffed and burgered enough of us in their time I'd say. Yes, I know it's about the miracle, but if you ask me, they're just gullible. A tale such as this sticks in your craw!

Long before I was a chicken or an egg, some German burghers were passing through this town on their way to see some old bones in Santiago de Compostela. I ask you what queer things folk get up to and they call us silly old birds! Well, they spent the night here in Santo Domingo and one of the local chicks took a fancy to the young German. But he wasn't going to shake a leg for her nor even give her a peck. So, she puffed out her breast and decided to set out for revenge. She slipped a goblet into his knapsack and then she tipped off the magistrate. Quicker than you can pluck a brace of birds, he was tried and hung for a thief.

His crestfallen parents dragged themselves to Santiago and pleaded with those bones to save their son's soul. As the chicken flies, the quickest way to Germany was back through Santo Domingo. They were of a mind to visit the gibbet where their son had been hanged and, blow me down with a feather, if they didn't find him still hanging there alive!!! Lawks a mercy!

Off they flustered to the magistrate to get him cut down. The magistrate, he's sitting down to his dinner and he doesn't want to be disturbed by the deluded duo. "Your son's as dead as the chickens on my platter," he squawks.

But, the chickens leap up, cheep cheep, and do the chicken dance! As if!!!! Go lay an egg! That's their story and this town's sticking to it!

· · · ● · ● · ● · · ·

From the nun at the guesthouse reception desk in Santo Domingo to the Heavenly Father:

Lord Almighty, grant me eternal patience. Help me to look favorably on these Thy quite vexatious pilgrims. They try me sorely and have tried me thus for many decades. Let me not chide their entitled ways: their incredulity that I speak only Spanish; their demand for instant keys, meals, and packed breakfasts; their dusty, clomping boots and scratching hiking poles distressing our fine floors; their insatiable need for clotheslines, wifi, air conditioning, double beds; their bedbugs, gippy tummies, and their used condoms.

Almighty God, I pledge obedience, but Thy ways are passing strange—why dost Thou send me these sorry excuses for pilgrims? They lack comprehension. Last year, a safari, this, a pilgrimage, next, a cruise. It is all the same to them, they are always on the move.

They think they'll find Thee on the road to Santiago, like some stray boot, kicked casually aside. Or, in a tomb in a grand cathedral. They're confused by nuns who scarsely leave the cloisters. Their dedication endures a month maybe. Are they so blind they cannot see a pilgrimage leads to the heart and lasts through eternity?

Oh Lord, here comes another one, pushing a bicycle across the threshold. Grant me charity, grant me patience.

Chapter 9

T he leisurely day had restored our spirits and helped heal my foot, so we strode out vigorously the next morning, walking through Rioja and into Castile y Leon.

There were fewer vineyards and more fields of wheat, poppies, and sunflowers. We coped better with the heat, out-striding the "Jolly Germans," whom we discovered at a coffee stop to be, not German at all, but "Delightful Danes." How could we have doubted this?

They were chatting with some athletic-looking young Spaniards and finding out the best beer establishments to visit in Burgos at the end of their week. A van jolted along the track bearing bottles of iced water, but we declined, having plenty of our own supplies. The way was far from easy, but we were in good humor.

We arrived in Belorado in time to eat lunch in the shaded terrace across from the crooked, ancient inn that was to be home for the night. Belorado is a large village, occupied first by the Romans but brought into prominence in the Middle Ages when, as a frontier town, it boasted harmonious relations amongst the Christian, Jewish, and Muslim populations, and defied the state by refusing to pay the tax imposed by Santiago de Compostela!

Today, tax dodging was forgotten as the day held great promise; it was July 25th, St James, Santiago's festival day and the Beloradians were up for a celebration. Our innkeeper thrust leaflets into our hands outlining the day's events. There were Spanish and French, but no English versions, so we were a little confused as I mistranslated "tirage" as "rifle shooting," rather than "lottery!" We spent a few hours wondering if we should take cover from the anticipated volleys of bullets.

It transpired that, in the early evening, pilgrims who had arrived on this day were invited to go to the Tourist Information Office to take part in a ballot. The lucky winners were to make hand and footprints in terracotta tiles that, once baked and sealed, would be set into the town's paving. Two women who had walked every step of the way from Le Puy, France over several summers were among this year's representatives. Their tiles would be interspersed with those of famous people, athletes, and politicians from all over the world. The whole spectacle, dance, song, and toe-tapping, heart-a-fluttering, music should have enchanted us, but it fell a little flat for, to our bewilderment, we were in the midst of a rare, actually unique, argument.

We'd been warned that this might happen, most likely *would* happen, perhaps often and with recriminations. People who know each other well and care deeply for each other often do not make good walking companions, especially on long distance trips. Typically, differences get heightened and resentments and judgments slip in. We simply hadn't encountered any of the usual issues: our strides were similar, we walked at about the same pace, enjoyed similar length breaks, needed silence or conversation at nearly the same times, worked through misfortunes, delighted in all the new experiences, and embraced this adventure with good humor. But we hadn't realized that, like everyone else, we were prey to the impact of prolonged effort, pain, the heat, a new time zone and sleep patterns, changes in water and diet, the stress of operating in a foreign language that we barely grasped, and dealing with constant change. My low vision made me more vulnerable to the stresses of the trip.

I had packed carefully, but hadn't fully anticipated the dim lighting in much of our accommodations. To avoid losing things, I had to focus intently on where I had left them, be extremely organized, and establish routines. Where was my flashlight? My glasses? My sports bra and least soiled socks?

I was also dependent on Chris to read me the directions for the next day's walk, what the distances were, the elevation, the points of interest, the description of the hotel, and I needed to hold this in my head or constantly bother him to repeat it, (which he did with great equanimity.)

Nonetheless, it involved a loss of autonomy that normally we coped with cheerfully, together. But, left unnoticed, the pressure was building. When, having carefully emptied my bags three times and meticulously searched through them, I could not find my phone charger, now this seems a trivial matter with wide availability of replacements, but it wasn't the case then,—we were both dependent on it, (Chris being a late adopter of iphones), and would be more so when trying to coordinate logistics for the wedding we were to attend after the trip—I snapped.

Chris innocently (but annoyingly) napping at the time was surprised by my overreaction. He has a history of perhaps being too solicitous of needy people, casting on the mantle of a valorous, charging knight and, true to form, went into overdrive. I needed to vent. He himself weary from the trip's demands and pleasures, needed to have his exertions and his sympathy recognized. Things spun out of control. For once, we weren't on the same page, the same chapter, the same library!

This was coming out of the blue. I felt humiliated, he felt rebuffed, confused, and helpless. After years of harmony, we did not know how to be with one another. Dazed, we watched the town's partying with vacuous gaze. In retrospect, for us it was a rough detour, a blip, something and practically nothing—a timely reminder that we are complicated, vulnerable human beings, caring for one another and minutely recalibrating ourselves to accommodate each other's needs. For a brief space, we had lost our synchronicity.

Perhaps we learned something, perhaps we just got lucky, for, in the next two years of walking the Way of St. James, we never had another significant disagreement. Others sometimes find that the intensity of pilgrimage opens and deepens fissures in their relationships. It was clear by now that the Danish girl we had met at the pilgrim monument a week or so ago had indeed decided her boyfriend was among those "things to be left behind."

Needless to say, we worked things out, and a day in the tiny but stunningly interesting hamlet of Atapuerca quickly set us back on track.

Chapter 10

A tapuerca was one of the Camino's most unexpected and finest gifts. I had never heard of the place and struggled to pronounce its name. If I had been a paleontologist or an archeologist, I would have been desperately impatient to reach Atapuerca for here is a site of unparalleled significance.

Potholers exploring the caverns of Atapuerca chanced upon some apparently human bones. This finding led to the archeological excavations that uncovered the "pit of bones," with bones dating back 400,000 years or, possibly, considerably farther. They uncovered the near complete skeletons of about thirty pre homosapiens species. Scientists have debated the precise species, but DNA analysis confirms that the skeletons provide the earliest evidence of human life found throughout Europe.

I found all this hard to comprehend, I felt as if I were stretching my mind in almost impossible directions. I had been exercising my imagination about the pilgrims of the Middle Ages, approximately five hundred to a thousand years ago, and that had seemed a stretch, but they could not have known as they passed through these parts that they were tracing a history vastly older than their own.

Notwithstanding its significance in piecing together the puzzle of human ancestry, the Spanish have done an excellent job of protecting the area. There was almost no commercial development, but tours of the excavation site are available on a fairly limited basis, and there is a guided display of how these earlier people lived. A little to my surprise, Chris knew a good deal about human evolution, so eagerly, we booked the display offered later that afternoon.

Even though it was 4.00pm, it was still incredibly hot as we approached the presentation area to discover that the tour was conducted entirely in Spanish. It was clear we were the only non-Spanish speakers, and the only Camino pilgrims. The others in the group had emerged from air-conditioned cars or tour buses, were neatly coiffed, and were equipped with battery-powered fans and ice-cold drinks in coordinating containers. Being perilously low on laundry at this stage and bearing our blotchy giraffe-like tans, they gave us the shifty looks normally reserved for vagrants. Yet, despite our unprepossessing appearance, Chris was to have his moment of glory and uphold American pride.

In somewhat random fashion, the tour progressed through a series of apparently ramshackle enclosures. At first I was skeptical, questioning what it was all about and whether I would understand any of it! Inevitably, I was so wrong; the rangy young guide leaped about with great enthusiasm, chipping a stone ax head before our eyes, cutting his own beard with a piece of flint, demonstrating the artistic skills of these earlier peoples. At every stage, he involved the young folk in the crowd, infecting them with his enthusiasm and energy.

At one point, he showed us the burial practices of the time—among the very earliest known to humankind. Reverence for the deceased body connects with more recent practices and suggests ritual and possibly a belief in a soul and an afterlife. Our distant ancestors would certainly have roamed far and wide in order to hunt for food; did they attribute any spiritual significance akin to pilgrimage, to these wanderings? I mused, but lacked the Spanish to ask our guide who was drawing us in now to the "fire house." He cast a spark on crisp, light kindling, and with careful nurturing he soon had a healthy blaze. In the darkened room, the leaping flames cast a magical, hypnotic, powerful, significance. *Perhaps these earlier people worshiped fire*, I wondered.

With the fire safely extinguished, our guide burst out into the bright sunshine again. He took us to an open field with a mound of hay bales. Within moments, he'd orchestrated the children into a hunting party, several throwing spears at the hay beast and then other groups closing in for the kill. Next, he explained that hunting methods had become more refined over time; spears and darts were sharper and more accurate, and the latest development had been to establish a launching mechanism for the spears or darts, called an atlatl. This new ability to kill a large wild animal from a considerable distance was obviously a huge advantage to our progenitors. Now, it was the adults' turn to join in the pursuit. The guide called out two swarthy Spaniards to try the atlatl. The darts thudded to the ground pathetically short of the hay prey. But then our guide spotted Chris, "Senor Americano," and motioned him forward.

The crowd's interest was piqued and Chris played up to it, praying to whatever prehistoric gods might be watching before taking up his atlatl. The spear shot straight ahead and plunged into the heart of the hay hill. Chris had slain the beast! He bowed again to the gods and then was cheered by the Spaniards who clustered around the ragged hero of the hour!

Trust creative, quirky Chris to connect with the people of the distant past and the dusty present at the same time. Perspiring with the heat, and, in Chris' case, with the fading glow of triumph, we walked back to the inn and found the Delightful Danes quaffing beer in the comparative shade of a limp laundry line.

Naturally, it would have eroded international relationships to decline their offer of a beer, so we joined them and soon were laughing together over our afternoon's exploits. Gradually, other pilgrims gravitated in our direction—two British hikers, a German, and a couple from Belgium. As dusk gathered, we drifted into the dining area and enjoyed a typical, and delicious Spanish meal of soup, pork, and crème caramel. I slept soundly and contentedly that night, but when I awoke before dawn, Chris was twitching and muttering to himself, perhaps dreaming of hunting the mastodon.

We rose to cold coffee left out for us in the dining room and to a surprisingly cool morning. Although the village was very small, we meandered around it for a while unsure of the way. We met an old man in overalls who was carrying a bucket of potatoes he had just dug up. Once we had admired his crop, he gestured toward a hill. We stumbled along until we really did reach the path. Then we noticed a few scattered hikers silhouetted against the sullen skyline of this moody day. Stronger now than when we crossed the Pyrenees, we reached the peak with little extra effort and looked out over the wide view that promised the city of Burgos in the far distance, and the culmination of our Camino for this summer.

The view, for those with good sight, was broad and deep and rather beautiful. Even with my limited vision, I felt great satisfaction at the countryside opening in front of me with an enticing goal in the distance. When I have gained elevation, I also gain a feeling of peace, of possibilities, of contentment with what has been and a welcoming of what is to come.

· · · ● · ● · ● · ·

As the gray dawn broke, it felt that we were walking toward a hopeful future. Yet, we needed to step out and embrace it. We had barely left the hilltop as the winds swirled and the clouds grew alarmingly ever more puce.

For once, we had to increase our pace to keep warm and to face into the wind and avoid being blown away. We reached an overpass and some distressed hikers whose bedrolls had freed themselves and were flapping in the wind, threatening to fly away. We joined in the chase and just secured them all when the rain began to torrent. Hastily, I reached into my backpack to retrieve the raincoat that had lain there since our first day. As I pulled it out, I felt the hard contours of the iPhone charger. Of course I did!

Immediately, I had a sharp, detailed, memory of leaving the hotel room in Logrono, almost forgetting the charger, clutching it at the last minute, and sweeping it into the depths of my backpack rather than its more usual home in my luggage before we left for the day. Why on earth had this recollection been so elusive in Belorado?

It was raining hard now with tossing wind and Hollywood sound effects, but the people we walked with were laughing, enjoying the change in weather, the new circumstances, and the renewed camaraderie it brought.

Navigation was not Chris' strong suit today. Yesterday, a hero; today, a mere mortal peering at a flapping, crumpling map and scanning the environment for the reassuring Camino arrows and shells that had directed us reliably for so many days. Consequently, we visited a couple of housing developments, some forlorn parking lots, backtracked, forayed into some graffiti-rich garages, finally asked for directions, and then we were in the seemingly unceasing outskirts of Burgos, glancing by the airport and gaining on the city by slow degree. It was rather unpromising as the obscure fraying margins of cities often are, but commandingly, in the middle distance, the towers of the cathedral rose majestically above the unremarkable car dealerships and jaded export buildings of the outer city. My spirits were high; we were in sight of our goal. Chris, on the other hand, was perturbed. His hooded head bowed down, he was determined to find the right way. (Hadn't we learned, in these last days, that contrary to the biblical "narrow gate," there are many Camino paths?) For some reason (the hood, the wind, obstinacy—surely not), he couldn't hear my suggestion that we simply head toward the cathedral.

So, we met many charming refuse workers and cleaners and osteoporotic black-clad women as Chris diligently asked for directions. He was going to lead me to Burgos and our hotel no matter what. It didn't bother me; I understood that he needed to try to protect and care for me and now I could see we needed each other.   Through a blend of luck and Chris' determination, we eventually found ourselves deep in the city center and approaching the cathedral. We passed a long line of pilgrims waiting for an *albergue* to open its doors.

Since they operate on a first come, first served basis, and this was a busy Saturday in the height of the season, many were anxious to secure a bed for the night. As we walked by the line, the first breath of melancholy brushed me. We were no longer of their clan. We had arrived at our final destination for this year, no longer pilgrims, but already tourists exploring the town.

Our path took us alongside the cathedral—a marvelous medieval architectural achievement. It was awe-inspiring to both of us, but in different ways. As a British child and young adult, I had been to York, Wells, Durham, Chartres, and many other superlative cathedrals. I was steeped in them; it was a little like coming home. Chris, on the other hand, had enjoyed a few brief visits to Europe, had sung at St Paul's, London, but related more closely to the Spanish-influenced mission churches of west Texas and New Mexico; for him, Burgos cathedral was as much a construction miracle as a reference point for a culture. Either way, Burgos cathedral is so stunning as to take your breath away. And today it was full of joyous celebration—there was a wedding and crowds of camera-clicking people filling the square. The bride and groom were about to make their getaway astride Vespa and sidecar—and in the maneuvering, the radiant bride never lost her poise or crumpled her dress. My heart embarked on some gymnastic flips of anticipatory pleasure.

We were traveling on to Devon, England and my niece's wedding, after this Camino trip. As my family is very small, this was to be the first wedding in thirty years! How nice to have such an occasion to look forward to now our Spanish adventures were drawing to a close. Once the bride and groom rattled away, we walked on through the town arch ringing with the startlingly accomplished music of street performers. The sun had broken through the clouds and Burgos was shimmering with energy and light.

We crossed a busy street and passed a small hotel from which, of a sudden, the Delightful Danes sprang, and invited us to share a farewell beer in the main square that evening. Having located our hotel a little out of town, we peeled off backpacks, gross clothes, reeking boots, and inspected feet for the last time. Mine were still beaten, battered, and blistered; Chris' seemed somewhat flattened by our exploits! We showered, dug into our luggage for cleaner clothes and the liberation of flip flops. The idea of siesta suddenly felt extremely alien. It was time to see the sights!

As I mentioned, we were tourists now with a beautiful city to explore. The afternoon unrolled, ticking the chins of statues, strolling through the cathedral witnessing two more weddings, hoping that this chance for love would endure, and idly looking for souvenirs even as we knew they would never reflect the glories of this journey.

At length, we began to tire and settled in an outdoor café with a glass of sangria. Surprisingly, in the way of the Camino, it was here that we met the only other American of this year's travels. She was a young yet heavy woman who had taken a long time to reach this city, but she was walking greater distances every day, avoiding injury, losing weight, and brimming with newfound, self-confidence. We raised our glasses in a toast to her and to all whom we had met along the way.

Much later, we shared tapas and clinked glasses again with the Delightful Danes. We were sitting in "red square," as they had named the plaza for its muted red tiles. Quickly, we were delving much deeper than the pleasantries we had exchanged on the road to Santiago. We learned of their hopes and disappointments, their joys and tragedies, and shared a few of our own. We were leaving in three different directions the next morning, but they wanted to stay in touch, anxious to know if we ever completed our pilgrimage.

· · • • • · • • • · ·

The scene changed, we were whisked to Madrid, the bull's eye of Spain, and then transported to industrial Manchester and, thence, to a North Yorkshire village—my parents, and better still, a washing machine!

Chapter 11

T he earth wound its loop around the sun as it had done for billions of years before the early Europeans from Atapuerca, as it had done for hundreds of thousands of years between their times and the presumed arrival of St. James in Spain, and for several hundred more years as his legend built and medieval pilgrims found their way to his shrine, and as it had done for hundreds more since the early pilgrims, until we began walking in their footprints. The Camino was like a telescope giving me through one lens a new cosmic context, and then switching to the other lens, jouncing my daily concerns into sharp focus.

One beautiful but blustery August Saturday, we gathered for the family wedding. Two mischievous terriers gazed down from an upstairs window at the top hats, the high heels, the feathers and the finery, as we mingled before the music summoned us to ceremony. Photos capture the bride and groom apparently skipping across the Devon countryside, witnessed by bemused sheep keeping their droppings, hopefully, in the sheepfold well away from the satin shoes and the whisking dress. Flowers, speeches, dancing, and the day was done. Well done!

Even though we were not quite ready for this, the promising doors of a new generation burst open and two precious little ones were born. A great-nephew and a first grandchild! Time to treasure the babies and let the parents change the diapers!

Later, there was another drawing of folk from far away to cheer a life passage. Chris' daughter was graduating from college and several of his family came from the west to celebrate with us and meet her boyfriend's family. No doubt, most commencement speakers aim to give valuable, memorable advice, but few succeed. This one did—not by yelling, "Whatever you do, do it in Virginia!"

as the speaker declared at my daughter's graduation, but because here was a man who, having lost both legs in a hiking accident, had spent his life trying to refine prosthetic limbs for other similarly unfortunate people. At the time, he was helping victims of the Boston Marathon bombings reclaim their lives. It was not so much this man's words, as it was the example of a life not constrained by misfortune that made the lasting impact.

Although we had our share of life's more minor misfortunes, it was a year without evident catastrophe, chaos, or heartbreaking loss, which concluded with more family festivities. In terms of international news, there was much to digest. A typhoon devastated the Philippines, most likely given deadlier force through the impact of the climate crisis. An Ebola epidemic killed thousands in the poor nations of Liberia, Sierra Leone and Guinea. The world mourned Nelson Mandela who had led South Africa down the path of reconciliation rather than revenge following the dissolution of apartheid. There were many conflicts and wars, a military overthrow in Egypt, and the escalation of war in Syria that included appalling acts including the use of chemical weapons. Terrorist movements continued to gain in strength with atrocities by Al Qaeda affiliates, Boko Haram, and the declaration of an Islamic caliphate by ISIS.

We shuddered at the horrors of extremism perpetrated in the name of religion, even as we remembered that the Crusades that opened up the pilgrimage to Santiago de Compostela had justified similar appalling violence and intolerance. The scope and complexities of the world's problems hung heavily as we prepared again to tread a path that offered hope and restitution.

· · • • • • • • · ·

En route to our second Camino summer, we joined with family in London to celebrate my parents' diamond (sixtieth) wedding anniversary. The Queen had sent them a card (as she did for all her subjects marking sixty or sixty-five years of marriage, or a hundredth birthday), but was unavailable to attend. It was her loss—she missed a musical, a good dinner, and even better company!

Chris and I both knew that families can be like dumpling stew, with lumps and bumps and gobs of gristle, leftover vegetables, and discordant herbs, but simmered and subtly seasoned—oh how sweet!

We'd been working on folding and blending our families for a good many years now and it was good to appreciate the rich, diverse mixture. They sent us on our way, with laughter, love, some shaking of the head, and some scarce concealed anxieties. Sentiments, I suspect, shared with pilgrims of former days.

Chapter 12

S weat sluiced down my spine as we entered the northern Spanish town of Hornillos del Camino in a shimmering daze of deja vu! We had returned to the same Burgos hotel of a year ago during an official Spanish heat wave!

We were excited to be back and, as I thought, eager to get underway again. I had forgotten Chris' need to mark beginnings and endings, so although we started early, an epic movie's worth of pictures absolutely had to be recorded before we could cross under the stone arch that leads out of the city. In the perhaps rash belief I could avoid the pain I had suffered the previous year, I had revised my footwear and now sported worn-in boots of different sizes to accommodate my ill-paired feet. One boot was brown and the other olive green as two pairs in the same color had been too much to hope for, so I felt as a minstrel or jester might have done as we passed through the medieval villages clustering the small hills that fringe Burgos and beckon to the *Meseta*. This is the relatively flat countryside that extends beyond Leon to Astorga, and was our terrain for most of this year's trip. Although we were only going to cross the northern portion of it, the *Meseta* extends south and covers forty percent of Spain's land mass. In the north, it's largely wheat interlaced with poppies and sunflowers. The *Meseta* seems to sigh in the half-forgotten hesitation of a breeze and exudes a blur of hypnotic golden motes irradiated in the sunlight. The waves of wheat are bewitching, but even this mellifluous magic melts into monotony after many days' march. It's a good place to lose yourself in time and space or to lose time and space in yourself.

It felt a little odd at our first coffee stop not recognizing any of the other pilgrims, but we'd barely gone half a mile farther before we met Richard and Phil from Ontario and struck up a conversation with them. We realized later that they were with a group of Dominican novitiates making their pilgrimage to Santiago in an effort to discern their calling to the order. Some of their elders walked in full habit and, during this year's hike, we saw other monks and priests wearing long robes and occasionally scuffed sandals. The morning passed quickly, our enthusiasm to be walking the Camino again fueling an extra turn of speed.

As we approached Hornillos, we caught up with a couple who'd been striding out far ahead. He was from Germany, had left from his front door and been walking for seventy-five days, and she had left from Salzburg and walked for eighty-five days. They said they averaged six to six and a half kilometers per hour. They weren't racing or trying to prove anything as were some injured pilgrims we met later; they had just built up strength, stamina, and a steady rhythm.

We lunched on hearty sandwiches bought in the town's main store, with homemade bread and cheese, local chorizo, and ham. Never mind that we were slick with sweat, rosy featured, and with matted hair, it was very good to be back in Spain. After lunch, Chris' behavior was a little mystifying. Over the years, I've grown accustomed to the minor erraticism of his creative genius, but this was downright odd. Our instructions were to phone our accommodation which was a few kilometers out of town off the Camino; they would send a van and drive us to the inn.

Since Chris knew a smattering of Spanish, I assumed he would make the call, but no, he developed a sudden interest in sightseeing in this fairly limited village. We wandered around aimlessly under the stare of the sun's fiery eye, admiring the unusual fountain in the square, until it finally registered with me. Chris was uncomfortable about making the call. We were a team, one of us had to do it, so, apprehensively, I dialed the number.

"Necessito Inglese por favor," I announced in response to the stream of Spanish on the other end.

The speaker paused and after quite a while very carefully enunciated, "Ten minutes."

And sure enough, after about twenty nervous minutes a van drew up at the bench by the village shop and we stepped in. Our hosts ran a few impenetrable errands and then we were deposited at our hotel in a nearby hamlet. Since we were so newly returned to Spain we couldn't settle to rest or read during the afternoon, so we wandered into the blistering outdoors. There were two farms, a locked church, and a footpath that dwindled to nothing.

We beat a hasty retreat and, as we approached our inn, heard noise coming from the tiny bar. We slipped in to find every rickety seat occupied by retired men playing virulently contested board games. What a revelation—a new occupation for siesta and one repeated in every village we visited this summer. Quite how these men spend the rest of their days and where they emerge from is a mystery, especially in a village as small as this one, but board game battles clearly brought passion and companionship to their lives.

Extracting ourselves from the bar, we met two other Camino hikers who had just arrived. Later, we enjoyed dinner with Jean-Francois and Claudine. My French and their English enabled us to have a long conversation. Like us, they were hiking the Camino over three summers, being also restricted by the academic calendar. But this was their third Camino and in between they were ardent marathon runners. They found the Camino's change of pace quite relaxing!

We appreciated the home-cooked food even though we couldn't identify the dish—it was possibly sweetbreads, but we weren't sure. To our surprise, the French couple drank beer and patiently explained to us how superior all French wine is to the local chilled red served in these parts.

· · · · ● · ● · · · ·

After an early breakfast, we rejoined the Camino and had a good morning's walk to Castrojeriz. We enjoyed the undulating wheat fields, the vast horizons, the metamorphosing clouds that dissolved into wisps as the sun rose, and the persistent background whir of insects.

Our minor injuries confirmed we were back in the Camino swing of things: my knees ached and we both had foot problems already. We marveled again at our bodies' ability to perspire; water poured off us as we entered this fortified town. Apparently, it was first occupied by the Romans, who used it to defend Galician goldmines.

The Camino runs for a mile down the main street, an unrelenting mile as we wandered down it searching for shade and our equally elusive hotel. We met many other sun-bleached pilgrims in the town; our favorite was a young German woman riding an electric bike, unusual at the time.. As she was traveling alone, we wondered if she had had any romantic entanglements, but she explained in what was usually flawless English, that she had the powered bike and a list of prior reservations because she didn't want "to be catched."

Our next day's walk led us, uncharacteristically, in the *Meseta* landscape, up a long, steep hill and then a sharp descent on the other side. As usual in the early days of a hike, I made it to the summit before Chris, ascents being my forte. At the top, we met a Dutch cyclist who'd ridden from Holland and was bound for Portugal after he reached Santiago. For days—no, weeks—he had been alone and now was nostalgic for that time when he had felt at one with the world, sensing the interconnectedness of nature.

By contrast, I was enjoying the communal feel of the Camino in this busy season, the sense of shared purpose and endurance. This was dispelled a while later when we arrived at an outdoor café. Somewhat comically we sat at tables flanked by sheets flapping in the wind and sweetly smelling of detergent. For no discernible reason, the people sharing this laundry idyll with us were almost all English, but no one struck up a conversation with us or with each other; all had heads bowed, worshiping their phones!

We walked on for several hours through unremarkable villages, serenaded occasionally by an Italian and a Korean whose party piece was Queen's "We are the Champions" complete with air guitar! At lunch, in a hidden garden café, our sense of community was restored with many people eager to share their experiences including a man who turned out to be the women's soccer coach at my son's small, New England, college. Suddenly, in the midst of arid Spain, we were envisioning the green fields and slopes and soccer pitches of Vermont.

Our next day's hike passed similarly in a humming heat haze of dusty golden countryside stretching out to distant horizons.

Occasionally, we were accompanied by other hikers, but mostly we walked alone. These parts had attracted mystics in the past and our isolation should have quickly prompted spiritual reflection. I had thought to figure out the issues in my life—how to live with failing eyesight, how to find work of service, how to strengthen my relationships, how to do more of the things that make me happy and fewer of the stressful ones. But contemplation isn't like a well-trained dog, coming tail a-wag when you whistle for it.

I found myself mechanically repeating the lines of "Twinkle, Twinkle Little Star" in my head, using the meter to beat out my stride. Time and time again. I tried to focus on something more inspiring, but "Twinkle, twinkle" wouldn't let me go. I speculated that it had me in its grip because the star is likened to a "diamond in the sky" and we had just celebrated a diamond wedding, my subconscious was making a bizarre, irritating connection.

Deflated by my own inanity, when we stopped for a break, I asked Chris what he'd been thinking about. Although he's never written a book, he had concocted the plot for a series of linked children's books describing a dystopian period. He had developed generations of characters and knew how and where the plots would turn and take shape. I reflected, it would have been better not to have asked him. So, with Chris' burst of creativity and with "Twinkle, Twinkle" chattering in my head, we approached Carrion de los Condes, where we were to spend a Saturday night. As we gained the town center, we passed a pilgrim statue discordantly strumming a faded, cracked guitar.

Apparently, the sign it wore about its neck proclaimed a free concert, but we paid no heed, probably a bunch of hippies or well-intentioned, but lesser-talented, rock musicians, we thought, and pressed on to our eagles' nest room perched atop a fading hostel that looked over one of the town's central squares. Being Saturday, the town was a jangle of activity with people bustling everywhere, car horns blaring, bicycles clattering, and people shouting greetings to one another above the hubbub.

Our garret was Spartan, but with a surprisingly pleasant bathroom. We freshened up and went in search of provisions for the next couple of days before the shutters signaled siesta. In a comedy of the grossly absurd, we went into a pharmacy and pantomimed our pressing issues with constipation. The other shoppers seemed very entertained, exchanging barely concealed smirks, as we blushingly clasped the product the assistant promised would do the trick! However, embarrassment prompted nature to go into motion and we never had to unwrap that private little package.

As afternoon drew to early evening, we ambled through the streets, drifted into a church or two, and then took up a spot at a terrace café. We were contentedly watching the people pass by, looking out for blistered feet, hobbling progress, support bandages and the aching bow-legged gait of weary cyclists. We also tried to avert our gaze from "Old Yeller," a disturbingly drunk old man who lurched from doorway to doorway loudly voicing his tragedy in discordant Spanish. I wondered what slings and arrows of outrageous fortune had led to this.

Our modest hostel didn't offer dinner, but directed us to a dubious looking café at the entry to town. My spirits sagged. It was the least appealing bar in town—but at least it hadn't appealed to "Old Yeller." A few regulars were propping up the bar, chewing matches and keeping an eye on the muted TV where men in fluorescent Lycra and spandex biked in vicious formation like a swarm of angry hornets straining to sting. Glazed eyed, we also stared hypnotically at it for a while before comprehending that it was the Tour de France. There were no other diners, but eventually we conveyed our need for food and a solitary table was set for us. There was no menu either; however, the "chef"—a scruffy young man in a mostly clean apron, came out to us and mimed the dishes. His shark performance was especially compelling, but I opted instead for what we could only describe as "other fish!"

Chris ordered "beefsteak." When the dishes arrived, they looked remarkably homogenous, a grayish oval of indeterminate protein surrounded by a rapidly congealing slop of tomato sauce. The "beefsteak" was definitely *not* beef, but possibly had porcine notes. Inevitably, it was not a gastronomic evening, but we had fun regardless. The "chef," now bereft of his graying apron, came and joined us. With smatters of accented English barely better than my non-existent Spanish, and with his exuberant acting talent, he wanted to find out if we knew the British city of Leeds. (We did.)

71

His girlfriend, who had passed through on the Camino a couple of years before, lived there now, and had found another man. His heart was broken (ripped out of his chest it appeared from his performance), he had to go and avenge his honor, the honor of Spain, snatch back his iPad, and then dump the girl (possibly in the canal—it was hard to tell, the acting had become frenzied at this point)! We told him not to bother—even an iPad's not worth that kind of devotion.

We strolled back, swerving away from "Old Yeller" and distractedly noticing that the town was remarkably busy; all the bars and cafes were in full swing. Wearily, we climbed the many staircases to our aerie, anticipating a good night's sleep. We were utterly naïve. Our room, of course, lacked air conditioning and the only way to keep it bearable was to open the windows to the night air. A thousand parties seemed to join us in our little room, the echoes and shouts of the Spanish celebrating a summer Saturday night—and Sunday morning, mixed with hiking revelers who knew that the next day's hike was one of the shortest on the Camino, ending in an obscure spot with absolutely no entertainment. Glasses clinked, bottles smashed, shouts rang out, music roared.

"Old Yeller's" disturbing cries intermittently wafted up. No sleep for the righteous or the wicked—which we were, it was hard to tell. Yet, Camino lessons had infiltrated us and we didn't rage at the raucous night. We were immersed in another culture, another life, there was nothing we could do about it; we may as well relax and get what little rest we could. The church bells proclaimed the new day and, unsurprisingly, we saw barely a soul as we walked out of town.

Chapter 13

The limp plant in the corner of the room was dusty, dying, neglected of light and nurture. From my ophthalmic throne, I fixated on its drooping leaves and languid stalks as the oblivious residents casually discussed my case. They were crumpled, their short, medical coats hanging loosely off the shoulder as if they might slough them off, a carapace of unwonted care.

I had spent an uncomfortable day in these consulting rooms, undergoing test after test. Over the previous eighteen months, I had become a test subject or, rather, an object, as it usually seemed.

My diminishing eyesight baffled the specialists and the more outspoken among them had begun to hint that there must be something wrong with the rest of my head. By contrast, one or two proposed it would all sort itself out given time. I was too inclined to cling to this dubious lifeline. After a day of prodding and peering, no one would look me in the eye, nor tell me what was wrong.

At the eleventh hour, deus ex machina, the renowned specialist, swept in. Offering no diagnosis, he ordered the final painful test to be redone. After this, he gave me a pair of magnifying glasses, told me my life had changed, and without dignifying the disorder with a name, swept out of the room, exit stage left. They pried me out of the bathroom, sobs still rising in my throat to ask for a sample of my fascinating DNA and, in an offhand way, explained that a macular or cone dystrophy isn't that common particularly in someone of my age.

Some of the cone cells at the back of the eye had died, leaving me with a blur in my central vision, similar to that experienced by people who have the much more well-known disorder, macular degeneration. I actually have no evidence of either the wet or dry form of this disease, but that was of little comfort given that I couldn't see well and was likely to lose more sight over time...

Decades had passed before we embarked on our Camino and my pilgrimage was not in expectation of "healing for the blind," unless you think of it in that simpering way some people sing, "Amazing Grace's" famous line, "Was blind but now I see," saying things like, "Don't be silly dear, it's not about literal blindness, but the more intractable problem of spiritual blindness."

And here I was, wrestling so hard with my tractable blindness on the plain road to Calzadilla de la Cueza that I did not see the colossus of a combine harvester advancing inexorably toward me. Chris pulled me out of my reverie and yanked me across a mice-filled gulley to the safety of a bristly field on the other side of the narrow road.

Lack of sleep the night before, and the meditative state that hiking can evoke, had finally allowed me to focus. I had dredged up that dreaded memory of the day of diagnosis, and let my mind linger on some of the difficult days that followed. The gradual loss of independence, the stifling of the frustrations when I dropped the ability to perform another task, to sew, read newsprint, recognize faces, drive. Amidst the foggy visions of loss, I also realized how I had come to see that neither stifling pain nor wallowing in victimhood served me well.

I had learned about healthy grief and the full embrace of possibilities. But, my hope in reflecting on my journey of visual loss had been that I would light on some new way of slowing or coping with the deterioration. However, unlike the denouement of the biblical stories of the roads to Damascus and Emmaus, the road to Calzadilla de la Cueza didn't cause the scales to fall from my eyes. As I approached the hostel, my mind—like my eyes—was a blur!

Intriguingly, medieval paintings of the road to Emmaus depict the disciples as pilgrims ignorant of the presence of Jesus because of their large pilgrim hats! Contemporary pilgrims walk, often hoping for discernment, but it was my experience that generally comes with hindsight after much conscious and subconscious processing has taken place.

We were early and ate lunch outside with a group of Welsh students from a Catholic boarding school. The school supervised this cycling pilgrimage to Santiago as part of its Catholic heritage. It was usually a bi-annual event, but the terrible train crash at Santiago de Compostela had caused them to cancel the previous year's trip. After a leisurely lunch when we swapped injuries with the assembled company (my blisters attracted considerable attention, but didn't rank with some of the bandaged and swathed shins and knees on display), we went inside and made our way to the room. Displayed above the stairs were Certificates of Completion of the Camino—the first we had seen to this point. They reinforced our desire to achieve some for ourselves.

Hanging out of the window later, at the risk of being garroted by the washing line Chris had fixed to the shutters, we witnessed a strange sight: groups of pilgrims running feverishly toward the hostel. They were as so many skittles pursued by a relentless black bowling ball of a cloud, thundering down the road, crackling with electricity, speed, and power. A few leaped into the hostel just in time, others arrived later soaked to the sinew, shivering in jerky spasms for the first time since their arrival in Spain. Viewed from the safety of our room, the storm was a thing of beauty; the obsidian sky flashed with lightning growing indigo, purple, navy, and eerie pale. The air growled and clattered like a stampede of incensed bulls letting leash their pent up fury. Majestic violence swept by and swirled back again and again, putting mere pilgrims in their place. Who were we in the scope of this bellicose eternity?

In the storm's aftermath, the mood changed. We had relaxed our intensity and were lighter, and even more ready to bond with our companions. After a hearty dinner that included meat and potato soup, fish, and dessert, we went outside with the group from our table. Two women from New Zealand, here to prove their endurance to doubting families back home, shivered violently as, incongruously, they lit up cigarettes in the biting breeze. In a bid to travel lightly they had shipped back all their warmer clothes, and now were clad in several pairs of shorts and skimpy t-shirts. Among the throng was an old, Dutch man with a long, gray pony-tail. He earned the nickname, "Last Tango" as he invited us to dance in the shockingly cold night air. A whole family was dancing somewhat self-consciously in the street; parents, a teenager and a boy of about eight or nine. Given that the child was so young, we wondered what they were doing at a hostel in the middle of nowhere. It turned out this was their family vacation—a week's trudge along some of the least inspiring paths of the Camino. Perhaps there were fireworks in private, but in public they seemed to be hugely enjoying themselves.

As we admired their progress, I grew curious about medieval children and pilgrimage. Taking the trials of the journey into consideration, I had assumed there would be no youngsters. But, of course, since the journey took so long in those times, there were births en route, and inevitably very young children would have been included in the caravan. It's likely that very few eight or nine-year-olds went on pilgrimage, but their parents often went in hopes of a miracle cure for them or in thanksgiving for such an apparent healing.

As we said earlier, such a mission was often the reason a mother embarked on pilgrimage, but men also occasionally traveled on behalf of their ailing sons. A girl's fate, in those days, was a lot less precious. These mercy travels were in the context of a time when infant mortality was extremely high. Some suggest that one in five children died within the first year of life as medical practices failed to cure many relatively simple complaints. Where herbal remedies were efficacious, the practitioner ran the risk of being accused of witchcraft, resulting in many needless deaths—both of the sick and the healer!

Children were highly vulnerable and thus a desperate, prosperous, loving parent might well consider pilgrimage to improve their sons' chances of survival or, should he succumb, of a peaceful afterlife. Since childhood was the most risky time in an age when all human life was precarious, miracle stories regarding children who were healed by unexplained, supernatural means proliferate. Burial sites near shrines reveal that when these holy places were relatively accessible, parents brought their children for direct healing or blessing. Poignantly, the many nearby immature skeletons show that healing was not always forthcoming.

Nevertheless, the Camino would not be bereft of youngsters. It all depends on how you define "childhood". In medieval England, a girl could marry at twelve, a boy at fourteen. The sons of nobility started their training to become knights between the ages of ten and twelve, and peasant youth were apprenticed at about the same age. Young men had to bear the burden of taxation at fourteen. Fourteen was also the age when a page progressed to become a knight's squire. This stage usually lasted until they became knights themselves at about twenty-one. As many pilgrimages were undertaken to secure divine favor for battles or in thanksgiving for military success, knights and their young squires, as we read in *The Canterbury Tales*, were frequent sojourners.

We embarked on our next day's journey sporting long-sleeved t-shirts and hiking pants. Chris found it all refreshing, but my teeth chattered until we reached the first coffee stop. The family and a group of young people were already settled there, sipping cappuccinos and swapping Camino jokes.

A woman with a long, blond ponytail and a bobby dazzling smile introduced herself, "Hi, I'm Lara, the 'Dynamic Dane!' You should have seen me racing ahead of the storm yesterday. I didn't know I could move so fast!"

It was about time we met another Dane—especially one who had coined her own nickname! We chatted with Lara for a while, finding out that she, like Chris, was a music teacher, but unlike him, she was unhappy in her career choice and was walking the Camino in part to see if she could come up with a better direction. Following the yellow arrows that trace the Camino is always the best direction for pilgrim hopefuls but, for once, Chris veered from the path toward one of the many small stone churches that punctuate the route.

Perplexed, I followed him and noticed a little gathering on the parched grass outside the building. We had stumbled upon a concert and were loathe to intrude, seeing as we were in our dirty boots, carrying clanking hiking poles and bearing battered backpacks. But the American hosts waved us into the sanctuary.

We hovered at the back, not realizing at first that the concert was one of a series aimed at lightening the monotony of the

Meseta. Beautiful Spanish guitar playing vibrated across the sunlit space. We were mesmerized. Time stood still as we were transported by the music; first to a gentler, pastoral place and then to a world of passion, romance, love and loss.

We had planned just to pause here, but the music was irresistible. We were spellbound and barely dared breathe for fear of breaking the enchantment. We stayed throughout the whole performance, leaving calm and exhilarated at the same time. It was Sunday, the day of blessings. What a simple, and yet hauntingly profound gift!

Chapter 14

Nearing Sahagun, I ought to have been paying attention to the *Mudejar* architecture, a blend of Christian and Muslim that evolved after the reconquest when Muslims remained, maintaining their faith and living in harmony with the Christian townsfolk. I paid no heed to this; I was excited, my feet were healing, and I had less pain than any other day to date!

Sahagun offered us a few minor adventures, the remnants of a fair, a stalker who trailed me wherever I went, a surprising meal when clearly our translations of the menu had gone far awry, and a midnight call from someone in the United States who didn't appreciate the time difference!

The following day, our travels, scented with the fragrance from roadside bushes bearing large lemon blossoms, took us to Burgos Romero. Scorched with heat, this was an unprepossessing little town and I wondered how we would entertain ourselves for the hours that stretched ahead. After much meandering, we found our little hotel situated opposite a busy *albergue*, and settled into the basic, but clean, room. Chris stripped off his repulsive "England" shirt, rinsed it through, and hung it in the window to dry before donning another nearly threadbare, shapeless, garment. I found a passably clean shirt and we went down to lunch.

Rejecting the café bar for its heat and tobacco haze, we investigated the terrace. In spite of the town's obscurity, there was a lively throng gathered under the few table umbrellas. It looked hopeless until we spotted Nikki, with two spare seats at her side. Chris had a little reluctance at approaching a young woman on her own—perhaps she too would be fearful of being "catched!" But, I had no such qualms and asked if we could join her. Then a wonderful afternoon unfolded in her company! Another Camino gift!

Nikki gave us a young person's perspective on hiking the Camino, living in the *albergues* or camping out, existing on a shoestring budget, traveling with a large group of newfound friends. Nikki grew up in Puerto Rico and with her boyfriend Carl, was walking the Camino as an act of gratitude that was perhaps the inverse of the penance a medieval parent performed on the Camino on behalf of his son. Carl had been raised by his mother and his aunt. In the last couple of years, they were both diagnosed with cancer. Fearing the worst, he had made a vow that if both precious women were to survive the first year after their diagnoses, he would find some way to mark his appreciation. Given the economic climate in Puerto Rico, although Carl and Nikki were both college graduates, neither had been able to find full-time employment, but Carl had worked part-time in a camping store.

Here, they heard about the Camino de Santiago de Compostela and determined that this pilgrimage would be their offering of thanksgiving for the comparative health of Carl's relatives. It had been a huge undertaking for these young people, and they were embracing it to the fullest, even though both Nikki's knees were heavily strapped that day and she had had to take public transport in order to give them a chance to heal. In spite of all the hardships, she effervesced with enthusiasm for this great adventure. Beyond the pain and the financial worries for such a long trek, there had been tremendous fun in communal meals, singing around a campfire, and mostly, in the wide variety of people they had met along the way.

Nikki and Carl had begun to see possibilities for their lives beyond anything they had considered before tackling the Camino: perhaps, for example, they would move to a different continent. As the afternoon wore on, Nikki eyed the *albergue* with concern; the available beds were dwindling; would Carl make it on time? And yes, he came striding in with two Australians at his heels in the nick of time. We greeted them as long lost friends; we felt so familiar with them from Nikki's lively, warm-hearted stories.

As the afternoon tailed to early evening, gradually more and more young folk arrived on the terrace, including the man who dragged a cart behind him containing his tent and supplies for the night. We had to wonder, how had he dragged this across the Pyrenees? How much sleep could he get in the heat and humidity of a Spanish summer? Even though our contemporaries cast us as intrepid travelers, how staid and tame we felt in contrast to these young adventurers!

· · · · · ● · · ● · · · ·

A couple of days later, a friend from home, noting our lunchtime Facebook post from Leon later queried how intrepid we were and how demanding this walk really was since we could be lolling on a terrace in the middle of the day. By that time, we had done about ten consecutive half marathons, generally leaving early to avoid the worst of the heat. These distances were quite manageable as the route was largely through the flat, magnetic country of the *Meseta*.

In the other two Camino years, there were many days when the distances were greater and the going more grueling. Our accommodation was pre-booked with the aim of offering us the comfort of at least a simple, but hospitable inn at each resting place and this determined the distances we would walk. As I recall, those two unremarkable days en route to Leon burst to life through the people we met and the conversations that sparked.

Raphael walked with us along a section leading to Mansilla de las Mulas. He was a student at Madrid University and clearly thought far beyond the math and economics classes he was taking. His grandfather was a Muslim who hadn't practiced his faith in a number of years, but was tentatively re-examining his religion in the light of his Western values. Raphael had been raised a Roman Catholic, but was trying to forge a spirituality of his own. He said he was considering the possibility that energy is spirituality, that people project a force field around them—their energy—which is perceptibly loaded with their values and intentions. He said all this as un-self-consciously as he told us about his brother living in Paris or his roommate from the Dominican Republic. Raphael wasn't sure what field of work he was drawn to—possibly something with positive ecological impact—but he was certain he didn't want to become "a robot working in a cubicle."

As he left us at a stark café zinging with floor to ceiling graffiti decorations, he said he hoped we would find what we were looking for when we reached Santiago. It's a hope fairly often shared among pilgrims, but the first time anyone had directed it to us. We were touched.

As we continued, along our road, we noticed a Buddhist saying scrawled on a bridge: "There are only two mistakes one can make along the road to truth, not starting it, and not seeing it through to the end." Raphael, we thought, was unlikely to make either of these mistakes.

A blond streak rushed up to embrace us as we were enjoying tapas at a café near the albergue. Lara, the Dynamic Dane exploded onto the scene and greeted us as long lost friends. She drew some acolytes in her wake; Eric, a first- year student at Bristol University in the United Kingdom, Sonny and (perhaps to his embarrassment) his mother, who'd earned the nickname "Mama Bear" from the *albergue* crowd, and several others.

We were a chatty group radiating enthusiastic energy as we exchanged Camino tales. Eric who, in British style, carried a rolled up golf umbrella on his back as he hiked, had not intended to walk the Camino. His European history course hadn't covered pilgrimages yet, so he came to Spain intending to stay only a few days to watch the bull running in Pamplona. He'd fallen in with a Camino crowd and decided to take his chances on the way. Luckily, he was wearing well broken-in walking shoes and had a fair amount of the right gear with him so, open to surprising turns of fate, he'd simply taken the next step, and the next and the next...

His steps were just a little unsteady as he pushed back the table to go and check in at the *albergue*. The others decided to take their leave too, and nominated Eric to carry the half-drunk bottle of wine. Passing me, he leaned forward to say goodbye and half a bottle of red wine gushed onto my "white-not-quite" shorts!

Flushing deeper than the wine, Eric apologized profusely and did so again every time we encountered one another along the way. I didn't care—this was the stuff of pilgrimage—and I liked

Eric for his spontaneity, his sense of adventure, and his lack of pretension.

Dinner was served under a trellis of vines with a view of a silhouetted storks' nest straggling from a distant steeple. The owner and chef of our inn, an erstwhile scholar of the micro-science of the pre-Jurassic age (you really do see life on the Camino), had introduced us to the impressive young couple we were sharing this lovely evening with. Paolo and Maria were PhD students studying physics and computer science. Realizing that the intensity of their studies was having an impact on their health and relationship, they had taken some time off to bike parts of the Camino. With iron discipline rivaling that of any hair-shirted medieval pilgrim, they had left cell phones and computing devices at home. Withdrawal had been tough at first, but now they were relaxing into the escape the Camino was offering them.

We talked and laughed together for a long while drinking in the luscious vine, the tiered roofscape, and the outspread stars over northern Spain.

Chapter 15

F ormed from the sands of ancient oceans, the ash of primeval forests, fused in forge fire, shaped by the breath of life force, tinctured by metals from earth's magna, spun with iridescence, hissed, and cooled in the still waters, shot through with light from receding galaxies, my pane of glass set in Leon Cathedral's east window directs the dawning rays into the sanctuary. Creation's light bathes this *Pulchra Leonina*, this "house of light" that is the Gothic marvel of the cathedral in Leon. What wonders has my pane illumined!

I recall that, built on the rubble of Roman baths and a king's palace that was converted into an early church in celebration of the defeat of the Moors, and an earlier less ambitious cathedral, the current edifice rose in a way that seemed miraculous to many of the poor people of the early Middle Ages who lived in dark, one-roomed wooden huts, steaming or shivering according to the season. As the building work progressed, laborers, craftsmen, and their families streamed into town. Some hauled huge stones to the site for the foundations, the towering walls, and the leaping arches. Some fashioned winding machines, pulleys, scaffolding, and ramps for the construction. Others stoked the belching fires of the smithies to cast the tools and the window casements, the hinges, and the locks.

Masons, some from far off guilds, with chinking chisel and packed muscles shaped and decorated the stones, leaving their mark, to ensure fair payment for their labor. Huge horses and straining oxen lumbered with heavy carts heaving the supplies to the worksite. Gaggles of glaziers worked their magic mosaics cutting, decorating and forming the glass into the translucent tapestries that dazzled, and delighted men and angels.

My light caught the doubting face, the scornful smirk, as the galleries of windows grew tall. Never before, they swore, had a building blazed with so much glass and shimmering light; it was sure to fall, make fools of them, and crush their livelihoods. Once or twice I thought I caught a glance of misgiving flick across master builder Enrique's face, but he had knowledge of the new building styles in France, at Reims and Saint Denis. He had calculated proportion, and load, honed his skill at Burgos, and now he embraced his vision of a new, gloriously colored and richly decorated cathedral.

I captured the glint of pride in King Alfonso X of Castille and Leon's smile as he reviewed the plans and measured the construction. Mostly, he convinced himself that this brilliant cathedral was to the glory of God, a glimpse of the heavenly realm, a triumph for the Lord, whose light, I filtered lest it blind Alfonso, whose fervor was often-times misplaced and merely reflected his own vanity.

In those early days as the dusk drifted to dark, I sometimes thought I caught the shadow of a shadow. A dark shape moving in the dusty gloom of the building. In the daylight, the workers were despondent, their efforts were undermined. Who was thwarting the work of thew and sinew? So they set a trap, lingering well into the night. By the light of their torches, I saw them circle the giant mole, knock him senseless, flay and hang up his skin, a warning to all who do dark deeds!

In time, over the centuries it can take for a cathedral to evolve, the other windows were installed, cleaned and renovated, and sometimes replaced altogether. From my vantage point I cannot describe all the glories, but visitors often remark about the windows of the north transept, the windows that do not receive light, representing scenes from the Old Testament, comparing them with those on the south side that gleam with incandescent light, spelling the scriptures of the New Testament and the story of Jesus, the bringer of light.

Another favorite among visitors is the rose window depicting a group of pilgrims arriving at Santiago de Compostela. How many pilgrim faces have I caressed as they found refuge and comfort here, pausing to visit the relics of Saint Froilan entombed in Leon Cathedral? Until the great northern movements of the reformation, pilgrims venerated Frolian's bones, secure that they would offer pardon for sins and improve the pilgrim's eternal prospects.

Shining into the sanctuary, I saw the impact of other movements, the sixteenth century wars with England and France that curtailed much travel, the eighteenth century age of enlightenment that questioned earlier beliefs, and I felt the great movement of the earth that shook Lisbon in 1755 and reverberated among our foundations. Despite the insight, skill, and daring vision of the first master builders, my casement was jounced, jostled, shaken, and twisted over time. Underpinned by the Roman remains, our foundations had never been as sturdy as would have been wise, the limestone of our walls, towers and columns weathered poorly, and that audacious design had tested the tolerances of the structure to its limits.

Attempts at reinforcement were often misguided. I watched, in the seventeenth century, as a stone dome was erected over the crossing (where the transepts intersect), throwing the building farther off balance. My light quailed when, in 1864, townsfolk and priests feared for their lives as stones began to fall from the south transept. Long after the great cloud of dust had settled, I remember motes revolving in the light I cast on British architect G E Street's appalled face as he reviewed the damage a year later, and his look of horror as he learned of the previous worry-torn architect's misguided rebuilding proposals.

Witness to kings and commoners, commerce and sacrament, to judgment and justice, to miracle and misery, I watch the ages spiral. Now the pilgrim tide floods once more through our great doors, sweeping in people from ever distant shores. What do they seek? They stand in awe, and in my light their courage also inspires wonder. Two more step from the shadow into my beam. Unlike their predecessors, they merely glisten; they do not reek or scratch. Fretted in their sunburned faces are the expressions I have seen before, the grimaces of the stonemason, the glint of the glazier, and the aspirations of all the pilgrim peoples. Perhaps they are Jean and Chris. My light will point their path west to the cathedral at Santiago de Compostela.

Chapter 16

H eavy vehicles blundered past us on our walk to Villadangos del Paramo. For most of the way, the Camino borders the highway and our instructions warned us that this was probably the least appealing section of the entire journey. Refreshed by our visit to Leon and its incredible cathedral, we didn't mind the drabness of the walk, remembering that pilgrimages evolved rather than being planned as routes of scenic beauty.

We were making good progress, sensing that soon we would emerge from the *Meseta*, a section often skipped by those who prefer the Camino's highlights or have limited time. When we reached the town, it too, had little charm appeal, but again we weren't concerned. This was a place where ordinary folk lived and worked, had their struggles and their victories. It was authentic, unadorned for the tourists and our thoughts turned again to the medieval pilgrims, resting where they could and being grateful for any amenities no matter how plain or unappealing the hamlet.

Our amenities were a simple hotel that had a surprisingly busy restaurant. A very elderly woman shuffled in arthritically slowly ahead of us. She was so slow that we tried to converse with her as she edged along. She laughed and smiled, but we could not understand. Her companion told us that, for over ninety years, she hadn't believed there were any other languages apart from Spanish (and its dialects) and she wasn't about to change now.

We were in a conversational mood and engaged the lone diner at the table adjacent to us. He, too, was walking the Camino (for the fifth time), but he was detesting this year's experience, and complained about it throughout the entire three course meal. He especially grumbled about the *albergues* where he had spent most nights of his trip. They were full of young people who had no respect, he said. They chatted and drank and sang, played the guitar, overtook the cooking facilities, used iPhones, had no idea how to treat blisters, traveled in packs, walked too slow or too fast, were late for the 10.00pm curfew, offered him snacks he couldn't digest, and flushed the toilet in the middle of the night! The more he talked, the more we realized he was referring to Nikki and Carl's travel companions and the more we wished we were lunching with them instead of this man we nicknamed, "El Misero!"

The day was uneventful until nightfall ushered in a small fiesta on the town square with dancing, castanets, and what seemed to be political speeches. "El Misero" was at the opposite side of the square—we wondered if he was about to complain about the local color and cheerful festivities, but we decided to give him a wide berth. We went to bed later than usual for a Camino night and expected to drift effortlessly into a sound sleep. This was about the time the restaurateurs ate their meal in the courtyard beneath our room. They ate with gusto and much cackling and shouting. Then they decided to recycle a whole year's worth of bottles, clinking and crashing into the early hours. About then, the "music" started. The noise was so violent and deafening, Chris reached for the earplugs he had carried with him pointlessly thus far.

· · · ●·●· ● ● ● ·

After an early breakfast, we walked out of town accompanied still by the throbbing music. To our surprise, it came not from the town square—the setting for the previous evening's fiesta—but from a mile and a half behind us on the outskirts of town. We were weary, but we couldn't help wickedly wondering how "El Misero" had enjoyed his night's refuge in a "quiet" hotel.

The route continued alongside the road for much of the way, but the demands of a gradual, but seemingly unending hill, reassured us that we had indeed left the *Meseta* and were heading toward the more dramatic and demanding mountains of Galicia. We plopped down at the crest of the hill and ate a lunch that included chorizo, cashews, and Aquarius, the Spanish equivalent of Gatorade. We certainly needed that fuel to walk the rest of the way into Astorga.

We were covering a larger distance than usual for this year, and the sun was in serious debate as to whether to melt the tarmac.

Eventually, we reached a long, low warehouse that cast a miniscule strip of shadow. We both zeroed in on this tiny bit of relief and simultaneously slowed our steps to make the respite last. Later, we both admitted that we had begun to feel a little light-headed. We were drinking liters of water, but the extra distance, intense heat, and the lack of sleep the previous night were taking their toll.

Beyond the warehouse, we had to cross a railway track via an ingeniously overwrought and clanging footbridge and then scale the ridiculously steep road into the fortified city. Although we felt as if we were going to dissolve into little pools on the scalding stone paving of the main square, Astorga was worth all the effort.

After wandering wearily astray, we found our hotel located on the central square. We were so used to scouring the back alleys for accommodation that this prime location baffled us for a while. My trip notes read, "Very nice hotel, A/C, elevator, hairdryer." I had my priorities in proper order!

The receptionist was rather strangely dressed, but with incipient heat exhaustion and relief at our arrival, we didn't register this for a few moments. Her loose white dress turned out to be a toga—for this was Roman festival weekend: the locals were embracing it whole-heartedly, and there was lots to enjoy.

There's archaeological evidence to show that the area around Astorga was settled long before the arrival of the Romans and that the district was home to different ethnic groups including the Maragatos people and, later, the Celts. The Romans faced stiff opposition from the Gallic peoples, who purportedly (according to the account by Paulus Orosius) gathered an army of 60,000 resistors.

Remnants of fierce pride in the tenacity of the indigenous peoples pervaded the fiesta with many of the townsfolk donning animal skin costumes in a rough approximation of the outfits their ancestors would have worn. Not surprisingly, there appears to be collective amnesia about the fact that some of the locals opportunistically changed sides and later fought on behalf of the Romans in distant parts of the empire!

As we ambled around the Roman market, I was taken aback to find an unusual kind of jewelry that was nonetheless very familiar to me. The highly polished black gems are jet, found primarily in Whitby, North Yorkshire close to my parents' home. Obviously they were also found in and around Astorga. Jet results, as unlikely as it may seem, from the decomposition in water, over millennia, of wood from tree species similar to the modern Monkey Puzzle tree! Monkey Puzzles are my favorite trees and I always admire the one next door to my parents' house, while my dad mutters about its roots undermining his property! Jet became very popular in Victorian England as mourning wear. Evidently, the Romans also prized it and later medieval pilgrims wore it in the form of amulets. Extracting and cutting jet is a challenging process that has led to many imitations of the scarce yet rather soft stone.

Wandering back to the main square, we passed a waiter addressing a *Jamon Iberico*. This is a specialty of Spain. We learned later that the pigs feed on acorns which have a very high fat content. This produces a thick layer of fat on the pig, which insulates the haunch when hung. The meat can be hung for up to three years, allowing a rich flavor to develop slowly. The cured pork leg was extended on a frame and the waiter was sharpening his knives in preparation for cutting it into wafer-thin slices.

He offered us a sample of this highly prized delicacy. It made a delicious appetizer. We settled ourselves for dinner at tables sprawling across the main square. Close by, there was a long table accommodating the monks and novices we had seen early in the walk. I had always thought of the monastic life as rather austere, a life of duty and deprivation. But these guys were having a party, talking animatedly, and jovially comparing blisters, shin splints and swollen knees. Once sweaty feet were skirted or tucked beneath the tablecloth, glasses were raised in a rowdy toast to St. Jacques.

Of course, to French Canadians from Ontario, St. Jacques is their name for St. James, and today was July 25th, the saint's festival day. We clinked our glasses and drank to St. Jacques, St. James and, as the Spanish know him, Santiago.

Timed perfectly at that moment, Lara, Eric, and Sonny appeared in pursuit of wine to take with them to the *albergue*! We gave them our spare half bottle, and they wandered off contentedly, managing not to spill the contents on me or anywhere else. Before dessert (chocolate mousse) came to an end, we heard the commanding sounds of an approaching procession. Leading the marchers were fine upright Romans, centurions flourishing laurel wreaths and greaves, senators modeling supple leather Jesus sandals and Egyptian cotton starched sheets. They were followed by the conquered peoples, an increasingly scruffy and disheveled mob, dragging their chained feet and occasionally hurling insults at their condescending captors. Bringing up the rear, the most unkempt, but also the most savage ruffians were the Franks and inevitably perhaps, the Scots whose barbarity had erstwhile caused the Emperor Hadrian to enclose within a wall. As the parade broke up, we noticed a father pushing a double stroller decked out as a Roman chariot, and a prisoner in a flimsy cage being dragged behind two fierce Roman soldiers.

As we looked closer, we noticed the town's young women had generally chosen to dress in elegant and very short Roman tunics, and the young men, bare-chested, had opted for the more macho animal skins of the resistance fighters.

After I had been photographed with three lovely ladies in mini-togas, heels, makeup, and flattering jewelry, and Chris with the young bucks in skins, we called it a night and retreated to the luxury of our air-conditioned room.

· • • •· • • • ·

Generous bunches of grapes, pregnant with the promise of fullness dangled tantalizingly above my head, stray tendrils from the vine twisted in my hair as I sat reading in the trellised terrace of our hostel in Rabanal the following afternoon. It was a delicious scene with shafts of sunlight filtering through the leafy arbor and flitting across the stone patio. My book (on e-reader) didn't really captivate me; I was more entranced by the beautiful timeless surroundings and my mind drifted through the events of the morning and skipped on to musings about the following day.

After dispatching the coffee and croissants offered by our hotel, we left Astorga with a posse of other pilgrims, many of them unfamiliar to us. We registered surprise until we remembered that

Astorga is the starting point for many pilgrims, being the gateway to Galicia and the more memorable scenery of the mountains. Before long, however, we caught sight of a rolled up golf umbrella bobbing along ahead of us strapped to a familiar backpack and realized that Eric and the Dynamic Dane were just ahead. We joined them, and soon Chris and Eric had engaged in a vigorous conversation about travel to Peru and its sacred sites. Lara's inner dynamite was propelling her on ahead, so I lagged behind and walked with a rather rotund woman I had not met before. I was glad I did not voice my suspicion that this might be her first day because as we talked it was evident that she had been on the Camino for a long time.

She chartered the history of her feet, from the swollen toes to the peeling toes, to the bleeding toes, to the oozing toes, to the blisters like gaping, screaming holes, to the rash she had developed from all the tape, moleskin, and foot creams she had applied. I winced in recollection of some of the foot pain I had endured over the last two summers of hiking, but mine were remarkably strong and virtually trouble free at this point. Hers were still recovering so she planned to take a break at the next coffee stop. Before I left her there, she told me she had witnessed many miracles on the Camino, but the biggest miracle of all, she said, was that she now dared to believe that she would reach the cathedral and complete her pilgrimage in Santiago de Compostela. Even though she rested at the coffee shop, her presence stayed with me for the rest of the morning's walk, making the heat and the sweat seem insignificant.

We had paced ourselves to reach Rabanal by lunchtime in order to have a long rest in preparation for the next day's challenging walk and the last hiking day of our current trip. The ancient hostel was rather lovely, situated at the end of the stone buildings that lined the steep road through the small town. Our fellow hikers peeled off at all the *albergues* and hostels at the lower end of the street, but we persisted unperturbed, thinking we would have the advantage the next morning. Poor Chris had to persist a little longer heaving the suitcases (that had already been delivered) up three flights of dark, uneven, time-worn stairs that presented too much of a danger to my low vision, to our room inevitably in the farthest upper corner of the building.

He got his reward, slipping into siesta after a good lunch, while I, a little more restless, strolled down to the luscious terrace with my book. I had a twinge of regret that I had not brought the information for the following day with me—I would have had to struggle to read the small print even with magnifying glasses, but I'd recollect better some of the finer points. Then my mind played its joker card, slipping into wistful anticipation of the end of this year's journey, how much we would miss the Camino and how far away next summer seemed.

Prompted maybe by the woman I had met earlier, I began to see that we were in relationship with this journey, weeping and rejoicing with it as we would normally do with friends or family. Time drifted by and, at some point, Chris joined me, quick to tell me that his snoozing mind had played the same trick and we were both suspended between eager anticipation for the next day's challenge and regret that it was to be our finale for this year.

Chapter 17

We heard the measured march of hiking boots and the rattling of trekking poles pass our window well before dawn. As soon as it was half-light, we were in their company, steadily climbing out of Rabanal into steep and glorious hillsides.

At that hour, there was a subtle breeze and the hillside shimmered in the dawning light. Small trees and bushes emerged from the dusky shadows, and as the light unfurled, we saw hills draped with dark violet heather bells. Small animals darted about in the undergrowth and soaring birds trilled in the trans cerulean air. It was as if a natural theater were being revealed to an avid audience, first the scenery, then the light and sound, then the supporting cast—were we the character actors or the audience? It was hard to tell.

We made a steady ascent and I was glad of it, much preferring to go up than down. Going up challenges the lungs, but is easier on my leg muscles as limited sight forces me to brake excessively on every descent, causing my muscles and joints to protest in pain. We chatted briefly with Sonny and his parents—his father had unaccountably joined them, appearing as if by magic, perhaps having arrived at Astorga a couple of days earlier. After a good climb, we came within sight of one of the Camino's iconic places, the Cruz de Ferro—or Iron Cross.

As you'd imagine, this is an iron cross mounted on a towering wooden pole. At its base there are mounds of stones that extend like a rumpled skirt showing its petticoats in wide circumference. Strewn in the mound and attached to the pole are multitudes of keepsakes, images of Jesus and the saints, photos of loved ones, and other trinkets. This is the kind of situation that usually makes me uneasy; I acknowledge other peoples' expressions of faith, but wonder if it is misguided or that they are being exploited in some way.

But here at the Iron Cross, I was moved. So many people, so much need, so many hopes. Tradition suggests that pilgrims bring a stone from home and lay it at the base of the cross to represent a burden they hope to be relieved of once they reach Santiago de Compostela. Given my predilection for a lighter pack, I had no such stone, but retreated down the path until I could find a suitable flat one. I retrieved a marker and drew a wobbly eye on one side of the stone and the initials of my children on the other. With some reverence, I added my stone to the pile. Naturally, I was not expecting to leave my sight or my children behind when we reached Santiago; my stone was an offering of hope. Chris also left a stone, never telling me what it represented. I was barely curious; Cruz de Ferro felt like an intensely private spot in the midst of a very public Camino.

We hovered for quite a while and then edged away to begin our descent, passing by stalls that would later form what was rumored to be a gypsy market. As we walked, the air hung with ethereal sound; we paused for a moment, thoroughly enjoying being in the presence of the pilgrim monks chanting prayers and psalms as they descended this Sunday morning from a holy place.

Quietly, we proceeded down challenging paths feeling privileged to be pursuing this pilgrimage, punctuated as it was with the interweaving of grief and courage.

· · · · ● · ● · · · ·

By lunchtime we had gained the tiny and beautiful village of El Acebo, and the sun had gained its searing unrelenting strength. The town hugged a track that descended steeply; the buildings were attractive cramped stone homes and tiny stores. I remember being a little amazed yet grateful that people still lived this way, especially as they were able to provide us with hearty ham sandwiches and Cokes.

We sat in tumbledown plastic chairs at the edge of the track as we ate, watching other pilgrims march, limp, or hobble past. Once we'd allowed a little time for digestion, Chris reminded me that we needed to make a phone call to our travel agents to let them know our probable arrival time in Molinaseca. A car would materialize there and drive us to the next big town of Ponferrada so that the following morning we could catch a bus from the terminus to Madrid and thence a plane home.

Our guidebook had suggested that we would be lucky to get to El Acebo in time for lunch, but we had had no difficulty so assumed we would make good time into Molinaseca, and we arranged the pick-up accordingly.

We stepped out in confidence to embrace this last stage of this year's walk. Hours later, we realized that our confidence was misplaced. The path was a precipitous switchback, heading steeply down, but lurching and bucking back up again in sudden jolts. The exigencies of the route and the heat sapped our energy and we saw several hikers droop by the wayside, being fanned by friends. I drank copiously—the water was warm by now and possibly no use in lowering my core temperature but, at the very least, I was avoiding dehydration.

The remaining kilometers took much longer than we had estimated and we were just wondering if it would be wise to call the agency to rearrange the car, when we turned a corner and saw the exquisite town of Molinaseca nestled in the green valley far below. As we neared the town, the air carried shouts and splashes as locals and pilgrims plunged in the river to cool off and let go of all kinds of steam. In only a very few minutes we were lounging on the grassy banks of the river, boots off, hands cradling a celebratory "end of this year's Camino" beer!

We hadn't missed our transport and even had a little while to appreciate the town we would reacquaint ourselves with the following summer. Chris didn't miss the opportunity to photograph almost everything he saw in his "end of the trip" fashion! Too soon, we were whisked off to Ponferrada, an indulgent meal, some good family news, and the realization that we lacked clean clothes of any description.

· · · ● · ● · ● · ● · ● · · ·

About thirty-six hours later, suffering a little from jetlag, I languidly watched those clothes make their circuit of my washing machine; the Spanish dirt and grime were draining away. How many more revolutions would it take before we stepped out once more on the pilgrimage to Santiago de Compostela?

Chapter 18

T he Horntail catapulted out with all the thrust of a space shuttle launch. Instinctively, my eyes squeezed tight and I felt a force crush my breath. The world plunged and spiraled, turned upside down and inside out, leapt and crashed and, for good measure, dropped precipitously; the wind screeched past and blood-curdling screams blasted through the air. And just when I realized I was still not breathing while my heart was sure to burst clear of my rib cage, the Horntail shuddered and jolted to a rattling halt. I stepped from the dragon roller coaster exhilarated to find myself alive.

Opening my eyes, I realized that the theme park was a blur; nonetheless Chris and I had survived. The "kids" (now young adults), joined us breathless and with reckless smiles,

"Didn't think you'd do that," one of them mumbled with a hint of admiration in his voice.

They had all been young when the Harry Potter books were first published. They had devoured the books and the films so that the "Wizarding World" was ingrained in them, and unanimously they had enthusiastically embraced Christmas spent at Universal Studios' Wizarding World of Harry Potter.

When all this was proposed, it had seemed tame enough; the worst I could encounter would be a boggart, a theatrical dementor, or perhaps a glimpse of a caricature serpentine, "He who must not be named." Strange as it might seem, the young folk had omitted to mention the blink-and-your-life-passes-before-your-eyes" roller-coasters.

We had strolled up toward the line unaware, lemming-like, following the crowd until we passed the point of no return and were clamped into the carriage. It was like this in life I thought, once the power of reason was restored, you keep going blithely on the same path without paying much attention when, all of a sudden, the rug is ripped from beneath your feet, and you are tossed on a new trajectory with all the roller-coaster jolts and twists and reversals. Events collide, helter-skelter, and all you can do is to hold onto an evaporating hope that fate will spit you out more or less in one piece at the other end. Such had been my experience since our return from the Camino.

One late summer day after we were back home, I was leafing through a magazine from the Macular Society (based in the UK), when I strayed on an article that considered possible treatments for people with macular disorders. One of the possibilities was to have a lens implant. Replacing a lens at the front of the eye may seem like an odd way to treat a disorder of the back of the eye, but in this case, the implant involved a double lens that would act as a telescope, magnifying the image received at the back of the eye, and thus improving the individual's sight.

I had researched this treatment almost a decade earlier, but after a call to the Macular Society had been dissuaded as they said that patients reported disappointing outcomes. But the current article seemed at least neutral, if not positive, about the procedure. Curious, I looked up all the articles referenced and this led me to other references, all of which suggested that the procedure was now effective. Tentatively, I called the society to discuss all this. Very carefully and cautiously, they explained that there had been many improvements in the last ten years and also that the procedure could now be reversed. They felt that the procedure itself had been refined to the point that they could recommend it with reservations. This is not a cure, it offers help that may be temporary as the disease continues to progress, and there were significant costs involved as it was only available in the private sector. Of course a little shiver of hope passed through me as I digested this news.

My daughter and I had already planned a trip to north Yorkshire to visit my parents at the end of the summer. It turned out I could combine this with an appointment at a London clinic to assess if I was a candidate for the procedure. It was good to have my daughter with me as the consultant rapidly explained everything. Had I heard it all correctly?

"Yes," she confirmed I had.

I was a suitable candidate and could expect considerable improvement in one eye and more modest improvement in the other. Could anyone who has suffered a chronic deteriorating condition for close to twenty years resist that offer of improvement? I couldn't, and with much more excitement than fear, gathered the necessary funds for the surgery.

Recall that as I regained terra firma after the roller coaster's death-defying ride, my eyes were a blur. Sadly, that was not simply due to the dizzying effects of being hurtled around wildly. It was due to two failed surgeries on my right eye. I still had the implanted lenses, but instead of the anticipated clearer view, I was seeing in triplicate! Eventually, after another transatlantic flight, the implant was removed and a single lens inserted as if I had had cataract surgery.

I was more or less restored to my original low vision and, believe me, I was deeply grateful for that. This procedure coincided closely enough with my father's knee replacement surgery, so at least I was able to be with my parents during this time. I returned to the Boston area in time to endure the worst winter on record!

As all this unfolded, Chris was struggling with his own issues. He has an incredible tenor voice and had sung lead roles in several musicals and other performances. As a music teacher, he uses his voice both for instructing and singing all the time. It had never occurred to him that, one day, he would open his mouth and only produce a gravelly rasp, but this is what was happening to him. For someone whose identity and livelihood was finely braided with his extraordinary ability to sing, this was a devastating development.

After a great deal of consultation, he learned that there were compound causes of his problem, including cysts on his vocal cords and a twisting to the voice box. Somehow, he kept on teaching, at the same time as trekking through snow-drifts and marrow chilling cold to a vocal therapist.

In due course, (after our final year's Camino), he was to have more invasive treatment and eventually experience dramatic improvement. At the time of our third summer on the Camino,, the recovery was far distant and uncertain. I was walking with rather more compromised sight than in the previous years and Chris was trying to banish his fears about his voice.

We couldn't help but notice that, like the Camino pilgrimage, our medical journeys could take on a spiritual significance. Does suffering have a meaning?

We were traveling with significant vulnerability, uncertain as to whether we would reach a restorative destination, and questioning our confidence in hope, ourselves, and our place in the world. We relied on all our coping strategies, routines, exercise and the prospect of the summer's challenge and completing our Camino.

Despite our challenges, the year wasn't all doom and gloom. The new generation added another member with the birth of my great-niece. There were birthday celebrations with seriously bizarre cakes, trips to visit family, and a brief escape to the wafting palms and glistening sea of the Caribbean. Immediately prior to our Camino we spent a few days in London for my great niece's baptism, held in the suburb of Wimbledon as the tennis championships were being played. London is a very cosmopolitan city, drawing people from across the world, blending their cuisines and cultures. Among the places we visited was Shakespeare's Globe theater, This is a faithful replica of the original. As the play began an actor came out with a censer to fumigate the audience, an echo of the great silver censer we were hoping to see at the cathedral in Santiago de Compostela. Our few days in London were an apt preparation for the Camino, melding as they did, the present with the medieval past.

On a world scale, there were alarming events—the suspicious loss of a Malaysian airplane, war and terrorism in many lands including ever deepening crises in Syria. Devastating earthquakes in Bangladesh and Nepal. The price of oil tanked encouraging reckless overuse and a rise in the threat to the world's climate. On a more positive note, the U.S. initiated more normal relations with Cuba and, a robot successfully landed on a comet bringing, the technologist, assured us advances that will benefit humanity..

The world's washing machine had turned once again and it was time to gather the laundry and pack once more for the Camino.

JEAN GOULDEN

Chapter 19

We met our transfer driver at the airport. He spoke no English and we were suddenly shy to test our broken Spanish, but he had a translation tool on his phone, so we knew we were in the right hands. As the miles sped by, we could see the heat haze shimmering across the countryside and along with, "Do you need a bathroom stop?" his translation tool also told us, "It's an official heat wave!" and when, via technology, the driver had asked how far we were walking in the next two days, the phone told us, "That is too far, maybe impossible!"

Undeterred, we arrived at lovely Molinaseca in the early evening, thrilled to be back and excited to get underway early next day. Chris seemed inordinately excited to see that there was a line of three windows in our room. He dragged me down the stairs and outside in the gathering dusk to admire them from another angle. I was amused but a little underwhelmed until he pulled out his phone, swiped through albums of photos, and eventually found the very shot he had taken a year ago when I accused him of obsessional last day photography. It was a sharp picture of the inn and the precise room with the three windows in which we were now staying. The year had turned and we were, in a sense, right back where we started.

We arose accompanied by a chorus of caterwauling cats and dogs' duets, and slipped out of town before breakfast was broached. I stepped out noticing that my mismatched hiking boots were less jaunty this year, muted by dust and distance. Even though the next two days were daunting, it felt so good to be back, recommitted to completing the challenge we had set ourselves two years ago.

We had left Molinaseca far behind and I was enjoying the rapid walk alongside fields of grass and poppies before I realized something was wrong. Chris was keeping pace right beside me; we were randomly chatting, sharing our pleasure at tackling the Camino once more.

His camera was safely stowed. I was not suppressing mild irritation at his ritualistic need to document every angle of this new beginning.

Progress indeed, I thought and began to lengthen my stride in relief. The respite was short-lived. Chris' mind, suddenly freed from photographic compositions, swiftly turned to his stomach! Anticipating the sheer horror of having to do without breakfast and lunch on this most grueling day, he led me well off track in pursuit of any shop offering edibles. No matter if this were a vegetable shop, a candy store or, even on one foray, a hairdresser's (did he hope for tapas there?) Chris was determined to find sustenance. He need not have worried of course as we knew there were many towns and villages on this part of the Camino, we soon found an excellent breakfast stop in Ponferrada, and over foaming cappuccinos and mammoth, crispy, collapsing, croissants, we made a plan to be at the sizeable town of Cacabelos in time for lunch.

We skirted the impressive Knights' Templar castle on our way out of Ponferrada, experiencing that familiar twinge of regret that there is so much to see and so much we miss on the Camino; but we were already apprehensive of the oppressive heat and couldn't afford to take a cultural break so soon. Instead, we walked on, exchanging greetings with two French women who had stayed in our hotel the previous night, and drinking in the serenity of vines strung across hills and undulating valleys; fruitfulness in every direction.

After some time, even the tranquility of the view could not distract us from the heat. *Had it really been this hot the previous years*, we wondered. *Had we become soft, lily livered in the last twelve months?*

Our slick shirts clung to our stewing bodies as, at last, we walked into Cacabelos. We turned into a little development that promised cafes and shade, but to our regret, very little seemed to be open. We spun around, dazed a little by the glare of the sun and disoriented by our incompetence at finding shade and nourishment. A voice called out to us, a man gestured at a table, he cranked open a canopy, then he returned bearing shallow, transparent teacups containing a tepid, pale pink liquid. We eyed these suspiciously and then threw caution aside—it was liquid and that had to be good on such a sun-scorched day.

We drank the strange warm rose wine, but doubted we were refreshed. The man reappeared with miniature *bocadillos*, the petit four of sandwiches, and offered a refill. We declined, but ate the mouthful of sandwich gratefully. It took some time for us to understand: we had strayed upon the visitors' center and this strange snack was a complimentary treat to any pilgrim passing that way. We were charmed at this modern interpretation of the traditional offering of hospitality to pilgrims, but neither hunger nor thirst were assuaged, so we hitched up our backpacks and explored deeper into town.

Feasting on ham sandwiches and Cokes at an unassuming bar we found in the town center, we were entertained by the bar tender's stories. He had learned English entirely by reading American comic strips, and could tell you every imaginable fact about comics, including the value of every first edition. He also plied us with his theories about how wealth destroys spirituality and how all this walking is fine for lesser mortals, but that running is the superior exercise. Apparently, he ran after he got home from work at 2.00am. most mornings—I wasn't planning on joining him.

Revitalized, and with topped off water bottles and the cans of Aquarius Chris insisted on buying, we set off for the afternoon's walk. The path led out of town along the margins of an unrelenting, steep, shadeless hill. The sun was brutal, blasting against every studied step we took, sapping our strength, and making us question our sanity.

As we approached the brow of the hill, Chris suggested we take the alternate route—a little longer, but with the dubitable prospect of more shade. Soon, we realized that the shade was a mirage and we had to reconcile ourselves to a farther incline with no relief.

Pilgrims sometimes push themselves farther than one could have believed possible, and this afternoon we were close to doing that. We were saved by a surreal, ruined concrete wall sticking up like some barbarous rotted tooth from the giant jawbone of the path, and the jagged shadow it cast.

We reached its haven and stayed there for far longer than it took to drain the Aquarius and demolish several sticky Werther's. Strange to say, I was quite happily slumped there, thinking that most people don't take vacations like this.

· · • • • • • • · ·

In time, we recovered enough to walk the remaining distance into Villafranca; we hardly noticed the charm of its traditional stone buildings and squares, but we did notice the thermometer above the pharmacy where the temperature registered well over 100 degrees. In true fashion, our map gave us only a very general indication of our hotel's whereabouts, but we found it anyway, and immediately noticed its lack of air conditioning. The Camino helps you focus on the immediate, and our immediate need was to find a sheltered bench and quaff a very fine and well-deserved Spanish beer. Having reacquainted ourselves with our luggage that too had been bewildered by the directions to the hotel, and carried it three flights to the close cube of a room we had been allocated for the night. It was then Chris explained his plan. We were to request "breakfast in a bag" so that we would not suffer anxieties (whose?) the following morning, and he recommended sleeping covered by a wet, clammy towel to counteract the heat. I was sure the sodden mummy wrappings would not work for me, but it was nice to have a guaranteed breakfast before our early start on another long and challenging day.

The early part of the walk was very pleasant and surprisingly cool as the road followed the river in a deep valley sheltered by the steep hillsides above. We made rapid progress in these early hours, reconnecting with the French women and recognizing some fellow travelers by their gear and their outfits; there was the Asian group, all clad in shiny socks, and several groups mystifyingly dressed in sun-sucking black. The path climbed out of the valley, regaining height and heat, but we were in good spirits and reached the *albergue* at La Hereias de Valarice in good time. We hadn't planned a break there as we wanted to confront some of the steep section before lunch, but we did pause for breath, and as we were strolling around, met Jo who was happy to chat for a short while. She was originally from California, but hiking the Camino the previous year had changed her life. She was now living in Spain and helping to run one of the *albergues*.

Walking the Camino had brought some simplicity and clarity to an otherwise overcrowded life and made her question her priorities. Fairly soon, she realized she was about to make radical changes, but she explained it was not a simple decision, leaving behind some people who had, at least to some degree, relied on her.

As we chatted in the brilliant sunlight, Jo explained that she had explored pilgrimage beyond the limits of the Camino and especially talked of a visit to St. Teresa de Avila to view the relic of her ring finger. Teresa, living in sixteenth century Spain, embraced the religious life in a time of religious and political turmoil. As a child she had been attracted to saints and martyrs and, as an adult, she had mystical, visionary experiences, wrote religious texts, initiated new monasteries, and worked for reform. After her death and subsequent canonization, her miraculously sweet smelling body was exhumed and pieces of it preserved as relics for the inspiration and, as they proposed, restitution of believers. To many modern minds, this is a very odd, ghoulish practice and I was intrigued at Jo's fascination with the saint's relic.

In our chance meeting, we had no time to explore her feelings, but it was clear that her engagement with the saint's ring finger had carried profound meaning. In medieval times, as we've noted, the church encouraged people to make pilgrimages to saintly relics, and indeed this was the purpose of the Camino de Santiago de Compostela—to venerate the remains of St. James. Visiting, and especially touching or kissing relics, was a way to minimize the repercussions of sin.

Presumably, most of the populace believed in the authenticity of the relics, whereas the church's highest officials must have been aware that few could have been genuine. Hearing Jo's story, I was thrown off balance. I had come close to ridiculing the worship of random body parts, but as she spoke I began to recall a rather different, ambivalent, yet tender, view expressed in the poem, "Reliquaries," by Mary Cornish.

> This is where they keep the bits and pieces
> of saints, in silver-gilded boxes
> walled with beveled glass
> to pretend that God's house is transparent.
> Here's a hair from St. Cecilia's head, cut
> like thread for the needle's eye, that unblinking gate
> to heaven. Here's skin from the wound
> of a saint who preached to birds
> in a dream of tongues
> as if winged creatures needed teaching,
> loved, as they are, by angels.
> This is the mystery I adore: the odd
> finger. The belovéd tooth. The blood-
> soaked cheek of Saint Catherine
> after the wheel. Even a scrap of the robe
> Judas wore as he walked the rose-scented earth
> on two bare feet with Christ, and leaned
> into the kiss. The sky is so far away,
> and the body's such a strange home.[1]

A little lost in wonder at the spell Jo had cast questioning the intersection between spirit and flesh, we carried on becoming ever more keenly aware of our own feeble flesh. Just as the track began its sharp, stony ascent toward Galicia, we passed a well-insulated man who declared, "This is one hell of a pilgrimage. I'm only in it for the beer!"

He hesitated before a sign offering "Horse Taxis," but after a tense pause he shook his head and began to tackle the path. For a while, I convinced myself that this path was not too bad, there were overhanging tree branches defending us from the sun, and multitudes of fellow travelers to encourage us on the way. The

---

1. "Reliquaries," Cornish, Mary, Red Studio published by Oberline College Press, 2007, Oberlin, Ohio.

spirit was willing, the flesh was waning, and as we had walked over twenty kilometers already that day, my flesh would only cooperate with more sustenance, so I called a break at the only inlet in this tide of trekkers.

We pulled out a packet of mass-produced mini-croissants, *saucisson*, and warm wax-coated blobs of gloppy Gouda. Chris fished for the Aquarius cans he had hooked in the mesh of his backpack and we rapidly engulfed the lot. Then we took time to watch the flow of pilgrims struggling upstream, slick and straining for breath. As rugged soles bit into the earth, I wasn't sure why so much water imagery was rippling in my mind—my "heart" panting for the cooling streams and still waters maybe. Ready to hike once more, we left our little oasis and continued the steady plod up the unrelenting path. Within a couple of hundred yards, we burst out from the tree cover, turned a few abrupt bends and felt the full force of the sun. Invigorated by the food and regular sips of water, we bent our heads and determined to climb this track. It was one of the most difficult afternoons of hiking we had ever attempted.

We had certainly climbed more challenging terrain together in the Peruvian Andes, but never when it felt hotter than hell. (*When did hell become hot?* I wondered, recalling that the Greek hades had been a shadowy watery place and that much of Old Testament sheol was dark and dank.)

Now and again we would find a scraggly bush offering shreds of shade. We would stay there for a while, scanning the uphill path for another desiccated tree or arthritic bush, convince ourselves that we had the energy and endurance to get that far, then venture out on the pitched path again. It was like a game of slow hopscotch—a lot of calculation and a little action. In fits and starts, we made our way up the track and finally found a tiny hamlet with café tables in a shed-like garage. We swooned onto the mismatched chairs and eventually ordered ice-cold Cokes. It is impossible to describe the pleasure of drinking those Cokes. Nothing comes close!

Following this unspeakable joy, the path began to seem a little easier and the power of speech returned once more. We chatted with Gabby and Kate, high school seniors from Tennessee who were traveling with their school group chaperoned by priests, in celebration of their graduation. As we talked with them, we reached the stone marker that pronounced we were entering Galicia, the final province on the pilgrimage.

The new boundary helped us to push through ours, and to make it up the remaining kilometers before our path joined the road that loops into the entrancing village of O Cebreiro at the top of the ridge. We paused on a low wall, catching our breath and congratulating ourselves on the hard days' walking and how wonderful it was to have arrived at last. In the background we heard the faint strumming of a guitar, as if the air was vibrating in subtle song. We got up and headed slowly downhill as we explored where we had landed.

We had reached an exquisite village perched on a ridge between valleys. Just left of the road one valley swooped like a swallow's dive steeply away; in the center was the village, and at the other side, another valley unrolled a little more gradually. If conceivable, the spectacular view was heightened by Ken's bewitching guitar playing and his whispered singing. We joined him just as he played the final bars and talked awhile with him, admiring the magnificent view of verdant valley and shimmering, infinite sky, before persuading him to play again. Anyone who carries a pack and a guitar on his back across the Camino can be guaranteed to strike a hard bargain, and Ken was no exception, offering to play if Chris would reciprocate. By now, Chris had caught his breath and shared a couple of verses of a song he had written about the Camino earlier in the summer entitled, "Along the Way." (It introduces and concludes this book). The singing drifted like vapor down the valley as, in the distance, we saw the faint sparkling hint of a rainbow.

As we strolled around O Cebreiro, we noticed that time seemed to be taking a good long yawn; the buildings are all of stone with numbers of thatched circular dwellings, and an ancient church, complete with its own odd relic. The place almost looks whimsical, but the lives the folk led were far from whimsy. For centuries, people have farmed the rugged land in some of the harshest conditions in Spain, living with their animals in the rustic round houses. Fortunately, our inn housed no livestock, but offered the inconvenience of a malfunctioning shower that only indulged my habit of drenching the bathroom.

After the dousing, I inspected my feet: the news was not good as I had feared from the pain I had been ignoring since lunchtime. I had a deep, difficult, near inaccessible blister twisted under and around my right little toe and other less pressing problems. I took some time and did the best I could to address all the issues before slipping on flip flops and descending the well-trodden stairs to dinner.

Overcoming some obstacles, such as the mystifying meal tickets and the incomprehensibility of the innkeeper who spoke the regional Galegan rather than Spanish, we had a very satisfying meal of rustic stew before wandering outside to enjoy the lees of the evening.

The village was overflowing with hikers, many of whom could not find accommodation and were resigned to a night hike. We caught many snatches of conversation—the man complaining of the discomfort of the horse taxi, the woman disconsolate because her Camino had come to an end, two students scraping their euros together worried if they would last the rest of the trip. In due course, we wandered over to the spot where we had met Ken earlier and gazed out over the valley.

Dusk was gathering in, but not obscuring the dynamic storm clashing in the distance. As we watched, gusts of wind sporadically whipped up and the temperature began to fall.

Beginning to feel chill and tired, we retired to our room, just as the storm barreled into the village, scattering tables, chairs and packs as it passed. It was a titanic struggle—hail hurled, thunder cannoned around, lightning lashed, and rain ricocheted from the paving like rapid-fire bullets. Chris stuck his head over the windowsill and pulled it back like a drowned tortoise. Eventually, hostilities ceased and the combatants retreated.

Spontaneous laughter erupted from the crowds below, many drenched to the skin, but many more celebrating the refreshing temperatures. We slept as soundly as spent warriors, and Chris had no need for a damp towel to keep him cool that night. The morning dawned and it was still refreshingly cool and we looked forward to a pleasant and significantly shorter walk.

Chapter 20

The going was much easier, generally downhill with, of course, a few abrupt exceptions and, given the cooler weather and the more realistic mileage for the day, we were able to linger at the coffee stops, and make more new friendships.

We enjoyed the Mexican family, a father and three of his children—he had six altogether and had taken the others on the Camino the previous year—walking from Astorga to Santiago. We had noticed this year's trio previously, looking discouraged and disgruntled (the grunge generation), but today they were optimistic and into the spirit of the pilgrimage. Olivio, another young hiker, walking with his parents and hailing from the Canary Islands, was also in good spirits, especially as he rounded a corner and met "Our Lady of the Pancakes."

This old lady, and modern-day saint, living in a very modest house, had taken the sustenance of the pilgrims upon herself and provided a continuous flow of freshly made pancakes. They were delicious and free of charge, but when Chris made a donation she hugged and kissed him with appreciative ardor!

After a steep and picturesque descent, we arrived at our resting place for the evening, Triacastela. It was clear, from the general scrum to find accommodation, that we weren't the only ones who had planned their trip to end over the weekend of the festival of St. James. As in O Cebreiro, there were many disappointed folk who had to journey on.

We journeyed merely up several flights of stairs to our clean, but rather bleak, room. Chris criss-crossed washing line from door handle to headboard, and we strung rinsed but still grubby laundry to steam in the torpid heat of the afternoon. He settled down to read the instructions for the following day, while I inspected my feet. They were not a pretty sight. As I'd discovered from the first summer, some hikers, even on the Camino, manage to escape without blisters, but most do not, and some (like me) endure a lot of pain in the process. This is mystifying to more sedentary folk, blisters sound such a trivial complaint; how can they cause such trauma?

Blisters form due to rubbing the foot against the boot or sock, or the toes against one another. Repeated abrasion causes the body to form a blister with its characteristic drop of protective fluid. If the rubbing ceases, the body heals itself, absorbing the drop of fluid, but if it continues as is almost inevitable on the Camino, and the blister doesn't properly dry out, the tender underlying skin is impacted and the blister grows deeper and ever more painful. Covering the skin is the obvious solution, but the blister preparations can twist or cause rubbing of their own, especially in hot conditions. Chris taught me the scout trick of using duct tape over the injuries and although it sounds extreme, usually it's a surprisingly good solution, having a shiny surface that doesn't increase the friction. But now I was encountering an entirely new problem: my right big toe had swollen. It wasn't bruised, there was no fluid to drain, it didn't look inflamed, there wasn't much I could do about it, yet the swollen toe was taking up more space in the boot and worsening the friction, thus causing my blisters. I spent a long time this day and every subsequent day ensuring the blisters didn't become infected, but from here on I walked in considerable pain. I tried to do it with as little complaint as possible; this was a pilgrimage and one was expected to suffer after all.

· · · · · ● · ● · · · ·

In the early evening we had an eclectic meal of tongue and French fries, sitting under an awning stretched across an alleyway. We greeted the two families and acknowledged other walkers, nodding toward the hitherto unknown single woman at an adjacent table. She came over to offer us the excess of wine that had automatically arrived with her meal and, thus, we met Mandy.

Mandy was an expert walker whose hiking experience easily overshadowed our own. On this trip, she had left her native

Australia several months previously, hiked a large part of the Camino and then, due to visa issues, she had left for the Atlas Mountains of Morocco, then England's Coast to Coast Way, before returning to complete the Camino. Since we had both walked the Coast to Coast Way and I had written a book about our adventures, we bonded quickly and easily with Mandy.

· · · ● ● · ● ● · · ·

We walked to Sarria the following day in weather cool enough to require long-sleeved t-shirts! We passed through fertile agricultural land, a little reminiscent of Britain—green countryside with a mixture of crops and animals. On the outskirts of Sarria, we made one of those instant friendships that are precious even as they are transitory.

A French couple was consulting their guidebook for directions to their hotel at the other side of town. Suddenly, we were in conversation with them, learning about their daughters (one of whom was currently spending time close to our U.S. home), their lives in France, the fact that they had to push on to complete the Camino before the festival in order to get back for a wedding.

As we left, the woman thanked me. "I don't know how I could have got through those kilometers without you... my left foot hurts a lot," she explained.

I didn't have time to explain that my right foot was walking in utter solidarity with her left!

"Mary, Jesus, and Joseph!" Chris exclaimed, revealing a long repressed Catholic upbringing.

I stumbled across the room to join him and find out what had prompted this pious outburst. Our hotel was close to the railway station and every train was disgorging crowds of pilgrims. They all looked excited and slightly bewildered, many in squeaky-clean gear, spotless hiking shoes, and pristine hats! Then, another train pulled in and more hikers piled out, and another, and another...

Back in O Cebreiro and Triacastela, we had thought that the Camino was busy, but it was nothing like this. Sarria is just over a hundred kilometers from Santiago de Compostela, the last starting place that qualifies a hiking pilgrim to receive a Certificate (or *Compostela*) at the pilgrim office, and hence is an extremely popular point of departure, especially in the days leading up to the festival of St. James.

· · · · ●· ● · · ·

Dawn's deft fingers drew back the voile drapes of day, unveiling the ethereal woods hung with cobwebs of mist and, emerging from them, an amorphous mass of hooded humanity headed west.

Hushed in the haze and by the inner intensity of our fellow walkers, we picked our way almost reverently among the trees. As the sun rose and the gauze cocoon swathing the misty woods evaporated, we saw the bright colors of our fellow travelers, heard their excited chatter, and began to notice individuals and pick out our traveling friends. Breaking out of the copse, we were joined by a new companion wondering volubly at the scale of the procession.

We had spotted him already, marked as he was by his unusual backpack that sprouted front pockets as well as those in the rear. Jim was good, and rather refreshing company since he had embarked on the Camino only that morning and had had no real concept of what he was undertaking. He had a company in Australia that distributed outdoor equipment and had combined a business trip first to Vietnam and then to Europe with an exploration of the Camino that so many of his Australian customers were talking about.

Australians and New Zealanders walk the Camino in ever increasing numbers, and although in our very limited experience they did not yet rival the dauntless Danes in their enthusiasm for the pilgrimage, we had already met a few of Jim's compatriots.

Entertained by Jim's guileless chatter about how remarkable this all was (and what a remarkable marketing opportunity it no doubt offered him), the early miles slipped by quickly and we barely noticed the annoyance of having to overtake endless groups of pilgrims before we could reach others walking at a similar pace to us. Above the racket of the throng we heard the wailing, yet strangely beguiling, strains of bagpipers.

We rounded a couple more turns and there he was, in full regalia, stationed not far from the one hundred kilometer marker stone. At first we wondered if a crazy Scottish or feckless Irish pilgrim had walked all this way in his kilt carrying the pipes, but then our brains rustily retrieved a nugget of knowledge lodged there when we had researched this trip.

We were in Celtic Galicia, where the pipes were right at home. Jim wanted to linger, but we needed to reach that hundred kilometer marker, record the moment, and sense that Santiago was within our grasp.

Although the new hikers streamed by, there was a little crowd at the site, all eager to snap photos of each other and wonder at how far we'd come and how little in comparison there was yet to overcome. We knew, of course, that what remained could still trip us up, but we had the confidence born now of experience to believe that we wouldn't fall short of our goal.

Regaining the milling, spilling crowd we were soon arrested again by a couple of young people holding signs explaining that they were mute. Most people passed them by in a hurry propelled perhaps by embarrassment; it was hard to know if they were genuine or if this public appeal was in their best interests, but we gave them some euros and wished them well before forging ahead through all the people whom we guessed were carrying their own covert challenges.

Having passed several coffee stops mobbed by clamoring hikers, we queued at the next and took our drinks out to the path where we met our French friends. The ladies, who we now recognized as Claudine and Pascale were temporarily barefoot, airing their feet during a rest break. I was impressed by the cleanliness of their feet and of the expert taping and padding each one sported. But it was best for me not to think of feet, my own were pleading in piteous lament.

As we were leaving, we noticed Mandy coming out of the gaudy gift shop, the supplier of sticks and shells to the uninitiated. The ostrich in the nearby field went by almost unnoticed as we were growing accustomed to a parade of surreal sounds and sights. We threaded our way through the crowd and introduced Mandy to fellow Aussie, Jim.

Distracted by their open-hearted banter, their immediate connection, and their colorful vocabulary, the kilometers sped by until we reached the steep descent preceding the steep stepped ascent into Portomarin, our destination for this day. We bid farewell to Jim whose scramble for last minute accommodation had resulted in a bed well out of town, and stumbled around under a scalding sun to find our more conveniently located hotel.

Liberated once more into the freedom of flip flops, Mandy, Chris and I were forced to linger over an unsatisfactory lunch served, or rather lobbed languidly in our direction, at snail's pace. We were in a forgiving mood, doubting if any of the cafes in this town whose year-round inhabitants numbered only a couple of thousand, could cope with such an influx of travelers, and we were entertained by Mandy's inexhaustible stock of hiking exploits, including the ten month trip she once took walking in Africa. During the afternoon's "quiet time," Chris read up about the town that we explored in desultory fashion once the sun began to repent its scalding apex.

Portomarin dates to the Roman era and was rebuilt in medieval times, gaining importance as a haven for pilgrims on the route to Santiago de Compostela. In the 1960s, it was flooded to create the Belesar reservoir and the hydroelectric plant it feeds. Portomarin was relocated on the slopes of the reservoir, with important buildings being transported there brick by brick, stone by stone. These included the town hall and the fortress church in the main square. It was cooler inside the sanctuary with its massive thick walls and half-barreled roof that managed to be both attractive and austere at the same time, and there was a sense that here one was safe from both physical and spiritual assaults.

We dined on a porch overlooking the reservoir; we were not treated to the local specialty of elvers, or young eels, but our pilgrim menu's offering of cod, asparagus, and the near ubiquitous crème caramel made a good substitute. People around us were in the light-hearted mood that places hugging the waterside often engender.

Several hikers, mellowed by the local beverages, speculated on spectral sightings of ghostly figures rising from the submerged ruins. We were not visited by wraiths in the night; Chris snored gently on falling asleep, while I tried to drift off with my feet elevated by pillows under the mattress in an attempt to promote some pain relief for the following day's hike.

Chapter 21

I n three days, we arrived at the brink of destiny. My impressions of those three days to Palas de Rei, Arzua, and Lavacolla oscillate—as befits an epic journey—between good and bad!

There are remembered snatches of camaraderie, finding Jim and losing Jim as he sought out ever distant accommodation, walking with kind and steady Mandy, cheering with the family from the Canaries, eyeing a group of beautifully dressed Brazilian women over dinner in Palas de Rei and assuming they could not be on the pilgrimage only to meet them again the following day, still gorgeous, but clad now in hiking boots, tailored shorts and fluorescent tops.

The less appealing memories include the grimy entry to a hostel, with the filthy stairs and the abandoned elevator reeking of stale vomit. Contrast with that, in the same town, the wonderful evening we shared with Claudine and Pascale sitting at a *pulperia* (we mistakenly thought this was a place where they sold only octopus but, in fact, the term means tavern or bar), watching as a waiter prepared street paella in a four-foot diameter pan. Chris and I were spellbound, noticing every ingredient, every adjustment of the flame, and intrigued that no herbs or garlic were added. We watched as passersby lingered, smelled the aroma, and often drifted into the café. The dish wasn't ready in time for our dinner, but a free sample made an odd but delicious dessert.

Although one of the hikes was quite long, for the most part, the going was relatively easy through the lush countryside that benefits from the cooler, moister climate closer to the coast. It was fun to walk with Jim and Mandy past a grove of aromatic eucalyptus trees and see their surprised reactions at a hint of home. Eucalyptus are not native to Spain, but were introduced from Australia in the 1800s with the intent that they should be used for timber. Apparently, Eucalyptus planks did not prove popular, but the species flourished in Spain and encroached on the indigenous trees.

On the last afternoon, teenaged Olivio joined us for a while as we walked through shaded, wooded countryside flecked with splashes of a more merciful sun. Later that day, I walked with a young woman who was heading on to Santiago that evening. She was surprisingly downcast and questioning herself for her mixed emotions. Her expectation had been to feel triumph, a sense of great achievement, pride in completing the challenge; instead, she was already apprehensive about returning to her messy, everyday life. Walking in her presence felt contemplative and peaceful and I had a sense that she put aside some of her wrestling anxiety for a while.

On the downside, I was walking through pain. My staccato, hastily scribbled notes for the day are dominated with stabs about my feet.

"Right foot, very bad."

"Losing toenails."

"Blisters on most toes and at side of big toe."

"Very painful."

"Even worse."

"Left foot blistered too".

Nothing was infected and I had plenty of supplies, and I could just tolerate wearing the harlequin boots that had carried me comparatively well the previous year. At lunch on the day approaching Lavacolla, I removed the boots and tried the sneakers I had stuffed into my backpack earlier, thinking that I might walk the rest of the way in them. After only a couple of steps, I appreciated the support my boots had offered, and reluctantly re-laced them and struggled on my way, being more thankful for Olivio and the woman's company than they could know.

Chris and I even debated walking on to Santiago that evening, so that I would have completed the challenge and wouldn't have to endure putting on the boots another day. Once we reached Lavacolla, (named because traditional pilgrims did their laundry there in order to arrive looking presentable at Santiago de Compostela), we shrugged off this idea, registered at the desk, identified our luggage among the bulging mound of bags, and installed ourselves on the front patio with a cold drink and the indescribable comfort of flip flops.

We noticed two unusually well-groomed young men who were casting anxious glances toward the gate. We smiled and nodded for a while—they were too preoccupied to spring into the instantaneous friendship that the Camino usually permits, but eventually they relaxed and we slipped into conversation. They were responsible for leading a Catholic pilgrimage tour with its twelve U.S. pilgrims and a priest.

There had been a miscommunication regarding their accommodation for the night and, since so many rooms were hard to find at this busiest season, they had gone on ahead and reserved them in the *albergue* attached to our pension. It wasn't clear where the whole party had started for the trip or indeed for the day, but their young guides clearly doubted that some of their flock would make it to Lavacolla.

The heat was beginning to drain from the day as two taxis rolled up, disgorging the party with the exception of the priest who staggered in about a half an hour later, wearing robes, hiking boots and a pained but relieved expression.

Finding it a little difficult to comprehend that tomorrow we would walk to the cathedral in Santiago de Compostela, to the goal that had seemed, for so long, beyond our reach, we retired early to get a sound night's sleep only to find our room buzzing with over-ripe flies. I watched as Chris opened windows, closed windows, wafted frantically, tried to swat and to fool the imposters into the bathroom that he informed me I could not use during the night for fear of releasing the swarm. After an energetic half hour, Chris was hot, sweaty, and bothered, and the droning torment seemed to have multiplied their numbers.

As Chris began to construct a tent like structure with the sheets, I thought it was time I took action. I eased my way down the usual treacherous set of stairs, found reception and mimed depressing a can of fly spray. The assistant smiled and nodded and reappeared moments later with the appropriate canister.

After the slaughter, Chris refused to open the window even though the night was cool. In the room's torpidity, he decided it was imperative to use the wet towel technique for sleeping. I rolled away in frustration, sure that no medieval pilgrim woman would have put up with these antics, but then I checked myself realizing that such a woman would have no doubt suffered far greater discomforts, sleeping perhaps in the barn or huddled with others by a hedge.

I was on the point of sliding into sleep when I felt a clammy chill; moisture from Chris' towel had leached into the bedding and was creeping ever closer to me. I rolled dangerously near to the edge of the bed but the tide of damp pursued me. Perched perilously in this way, I had been awake for hours when a gray, cool morning dawned and Chris finally rubbed his eyes after a solid night's sleep!

Chapter 22

I t had rained a little on our departure day and now, as if to bookend the trip, we walked below somber, drizzling skies. Chris sped ahead so he could film me on this last day. It's not the most riveting sequence, I limp on, a little pale but clearly determined as I approach the suburbs of Santiago de Compostela. We negotiate the traffic as the roads become busier and busier and the pilgrim tide swells. We know we are almost there, but for a little while longer the cathedral is illusory.

We are in narrow streets surrounded by tall buildings, Chris steps ahead again down a set of centuries' worn stone steps that are dim and quite tricky for me to negotiate, given my unreliable eyesight. I feel just a hint of frustration rising. I have come too far to fall down the final stairs. Tentatively, I make it, turn at the foot of the flight, and look up.

The world weary façade of the cathedral, splinted with scaffolding and bandaged in dust sheets meets my eyes. Somehow I am not disappointed. My weary, injured body communes with the broken stones. This spiritually inspiring and reassuring sanctuary today is bowed, broken, like me and like the people who gather here from across the continents. The square is large but strangely quiet in spite of the pilgrims who gather. There is an intimate, personal feel to this public space. It is as if the cathedral and I need to take a moment to acknowledge one another, to take a breath before the relief and excitement set in. In a sense, we have each been waiting for the other.

I kissed the ground. I do not know why I did this, I felt a little self-conscious as if I were playing at pope, but I had a need to meet the moment in ritual and this is what first came to mind. The second ritual was much more prosaic: I took off the boots—and, yes, my foot was bleeding through the sock. Chris, who had been lingering, transfixed in his own way, noticed and reached for his camera.

And so the spell was broken, we started to pose, wave hiking poles and hats. Others gathered and we exchanged cameras—it was time to record our achievement. There was also just time to line up at the pilgrim office to get our credentials, bearing our names inscribed in Latin, proof at least to classical scholars that we had completed our Camino, reached our goal, before we returned to the cathedral for the pilgrim mass.

We had planned to be in Santiago on this weekend to celebrate the festival of St. James and also because there would be more opportunities to see the giant censer swung down the nave of the cathedral. This regularly happens on Sundays, festival days, when any individual or organization makes a special donation and, since 2013, on Friday evenings. Now it was noon on Friday, and although the town was electric in expectation, the festival was not yet underway and hence there was no guarantee that the *botafumeiro (censer)*, would swing..

We enjoyed the service, noting that the American priest who had hobbled into Lavacolla the previous evening was invited to take part. It was also fun to hear prayers of gratitude for pilgrims who had arrived that day, including Americans who started at St. Jean Pied de Port. There were probably many in the congregation who answered that description, yet still we cherished the recognition. The service came to an end sans censer and we smiled at one another pleased that we had afforded ourselves other opportunities to witness it.

As we walked down the stairs, we noticed a woman begging for money. Chris gave her the cash he had that was accessible, and feeling that this was ungenerous added a Werther's Original candy. I'd wager the broad smile the woman flashed at us was as much in acknowledgement of the treat than of the money. It appeared Chris had understood something about Camino hospitality.

It took a little time in our air-conditioned hotel to effect the outward transformation from pilgrim to tourist, but we emerged that afternoon, showered and in the cleanest clothes we could muster to sample the delights of this lovely place.

After meandering for a while, we installed ourselves at a street café adjacent to the main cathedral square. In both European and satiated pilgrim style, we lingered for hours, witnessing the throb and thrum of the city. People streamed by, the stream of pilgrims, tourists and locals rushing to tidal wave proportions and the energy they generated crackled with electric anticipation.

In the neighboring square, the drums and pipes were limbering up. A group from one balcony would initiate a haunting, insistent, Celtic rhythm to be answered from another balcony, echoed and repeated with growing power and passion. The call and response of the music leaped into the air and you would swear you could see the soundwaves hurtling across the courtyard.

It was vibrant, hopeful, passionate, music asserting the strength and independence of Galicia's cultural, spiritual and political, inheritance, on the eve of the saint's festival and Galicia's national day.

At night, the air vibrated in a different way with the clash and boom, the fizz and crackle, the tension and exclamation of fireworks. Being unable to see at night, I don't usually go to firework displays, but Chris had found a way to keep me safe, and it was a glorious celebration, that over-spilling exuberance that often people from the north and west repress in polite restraint.

As petals of descending ash kissed our clothes we struggled back to the hotel mindful that the party would run throughout the night.

· · · · ● · ● · · · ·

St. James Day: the sun shone illuminating a clear blue sky and highlighting the grandiose facade of the imposing cathedral. The present cathedral combines early Romanesque elements with later Baroque and Gothic influences. It lacks the elegant airiness of Burgos or Leon, but the collision of styles is serendipitous giving it its own magnificence.

We made our way to the square along with many thousands of others who clustered on the steps, hoping to make their way inside to celebrate mass. Initially, the crowd was cheerful, calling out to old friends, making space for family to join them, but its numbers grew ever denser, so all thought of personal space was gone and we were packed body to body separated only by our clothing and our waning inhibitions.

As the minutes ticked by and only the faintest trickle of people had been admitted, the crowd's collective mood grew mutinous. A tour party, perhaps from a cruise such as the one my parents had enjoyed all those years ago, was allowed to skip the line. Insults were hurled, jostling became hostile, even the police, too casually supervising the mob, were accused. The gentle air rippled with the prospect of violence. Crushed as we were by the press of bodies and separated by the irresistible movement of the crowd and fearing that all was lost, Chris and I couldn't help but notice the irony of a mob of incensed folk frustrated by the fact that they were being denied a service celebrating peace and harmony.

Time ticked inexorably by and it was clear we would miss mass and the chance to witness the giant censer once more. As the crowd dispersed, we were simply glad it had not turned uglier, and set off to watch regional dancing and to find an extremely good paella, sprinkled with barnacle feet!

After lunch, we made our way once more to the Portico of Glory and entered the almost empty cathedral. Fortunately, we enjoyed the peaceful, calm, atmosphere as we had decided to stay here for several hours, to ensure our place at the 7 p.m. mass and our long-awaited experience of the swooping *botafumeiro*.

Having gazed once more at the resplendent high altar and the contrastingly simple rounded vault of the ceiling, we settled down in pews at the side aisle that we knew would provide us a good view of the censer. We witnessed several subsidiary masses and, although they were in a mixture of Spanish and Latin, it was evident that the priest was offering the same homily at each!

At one point, Jim found us and we had a reunion before he needed to head to the airport to return to Australia. I wondered, over the centuries, how often pilgrims had bidden each other farewell in this place. After all the hustle and bustle, the exertion and the heat, the continuous stimulation and variety, it was restorative simply to sit and observe, to pray a little and muse on all that this cathedral had witnessed. There was the day five hundred years or so ago when Catherine of Aragon had attended mass here on her way to England to marry, first Arthur and then, after his untimely death, Henry VIII. It was her inability to produce a son that provoked Henry to break away from the Catholic church in order to divorce her. Students of Tudor England will recall that although he married five other wives, none of them gave birth to a boy, possibly because Henry infected them with syphilis. All that was ahead for courageous Catherine praying piously in her pew as the *botafumeiro* loosed its restraints and flew through the cathedral window. And there was the day during the French occupation when Napoleon's soldiers decided to stea; the grand, silver *botafumeiro*. Or all the other days when ordinary folk had gathered here, hoping that their prayers would soar as the incense to the divine breast.

And so the hours slipped by, this time of simplicity seemingly the cathedral's gift to us. Gradually people joined us and we became aware of the great swell and surge of the congregation, though their voices were muffled in anticipation. People shuffled into our pew and soon we were crammed at the end, aware that some folk were standing in the side chapels and clustered around the doors. Organ music swirled through the arches and the aisles enveloping us and the solemn procession began.

As the ritual proceeded, I felt as if I were being sketched into a vast mural, one tiny dot, one pixel, blended into the grand screen of history, utterly dependent upon all the other tiny dots, and coming together regardless of many blemishes, to proclaim an epic tale. Wrapped in music, chanting, the reverence of priest and people, I felt as if the mass were seeping into me through every pore. I wanted it to go on and on. Then the organ rang out with the apostle's anthem, the exquisite choir sang, and eight monks dressed in red stepped to the crossing.

The *botafumeiro* was hoisted, hypnotically high under the central dome like a flashing comet about to streak across the sky. And then it flew, swooping down along the transept and sweeping up to the roof like a giant, looping pendulum. As it beat its steady pulse, it shed gusts of incense that drifted among us, then gathered and wafted up in aromatic clouds. Sound, smell and motion, were both mesmeric and breathtaking; the congregants, even those desperately recording the spectacle, were in awe. At last the giant swing slowed, the music hushed and we all breathed again, realizing we had been holding our collective breath. I felt the catharsis of simultaneous joy and exhaustion. I realized that my face was wet. I didn't know I had been crying. I had been overtaken by beauty.

We drifted out and down the cathedral steps, dazed, stunned and very content.

Then we turned and looked back at the great entry, framed by the softening light of the evening sky. Three years, five hundred miles and a great deal of effort and courage: it had all been worthwhile. We had walked the Camino de Santiago de Compostela, it had seeped into body and soul; we would never forget it.

Epilogue

Ultreia - "going beyond"

... Until one day you find the end
You've sought along the way
And pass beyond while singing
"Ultreia" at close of day

And follow in eternity
What led you here today
The pilgrim congregation
Flowing gently to the sea
Along the way[1]

Although we had reached the cathedral, the climactic moment when the censer stole our breath away, opened our hearts, loosed our tears, we were not quite done with this adventure. After another day of tourism, souvenir shopping, ambling around the festival fairground, indulging in more local delicacies, and simply enjoying having reached our primary goal, we journeyed on.

A relatively few hikers opt to carry on to Finisterre, to the sea and all its mysteries, and this was especially appealing to Chris who had not simply cherished, as I had, the dream of many years' duration of witnessing the *botafumeiro* in celebration of a completed pilgrimage. He had enjoyed it tremendously and we

---

1. From "Along the Way" lyrics and music by Chris Porth. Visit tomuzy.com to hear the entire song.

loved having this wonderful shared experience, but even though Chris had grown up in a land-locked part of Texas, the infinitude of the ocean was calling out to him, stirring up the memories of when we had had the great satisfaction of walking from one coast to another across northern England on Wainwright's Coast to Coast Way.

Back in our New England home, we had planned to hike this last section, reasoning that we would be extremely fit and undaunted by these extra ninety kilometers, but once in Santiago de Compostela our attitude had shifted a little. First, we already thought of ourselves as hikers, no longer pilgrims, and a little of our intensity had evaporated with the completion of the main pilgrimage. The route to Finisterre is also classified as a pilgrimage and there's ample evidence that Christian pilgrims have walked this way over the centuries yet, if anything, we felt a greater kinship with the pagans for whom this was a sacred journey to reverence the sun that died over the brink of the world. Second, my feet had still not healed and seemed to have developed a violent aversion to the hiking boots, and third, the weather deteriorated to the chilly, rainy days that can sometimes characterize coastal Galicia even in the summertime.

For three days, we hiked, rode the bus, and Chris even called a taxi (no longer having inhibitions about speaking Spanish over the phone), to transport us to our destinations. In better weather, I am sure Chris would have preferred to have hiked the whole way, but we no longer felt the challenge to suffer every step, particularly the day when we detoured to Muxia in howling gales and driving rain. Although I was wistful for the Caribbean and a palm tree idly wafting in a gentle breeze, I couldn't but concede that the conditions had a fitting wild beauty of their own. As we shivered in the porch of the simple stone church on the headland, we looked out through the clinging mist to the monument recently erected. It's a startling sight, an upright slab of rock cleaved by a lightning scar.

This was erected to mark the storm on Christmas Day 2013 when the little church was struck by lightning and nearly consumed by fire. As you peer out to the bucking ocean, your gaze drifts over the rock formations that tug at your memory—are these the rocks that resemble the sails of the virgin's legendary stone boat?

· · · · • · • · • · ·

The rinsed world glistened fresh and fertile on our final day, a day that felt like a rebirth, a baptism into a new life. We were keen to hike the fifteen kilometers or so from the town of Cee, much of it along the coastline, before the path dips and emerges on the beach fringing Finisterre. Many pilgrims stop here, discard most everything and plunge into the sea, playful as seals, in a romp of freedom, purification and joy, but we carried on walking into this fishing port that feeds on tourism as much as the ocean feeds it. We found a safe place to store the backpacks and I slipped into flip-flops for the final, liberating walk to the lighthouse, the cape, and the end of the world! We were light-hearted, no longer harboring the tinge of regret with which we had approached Santiago and the resolution of our dreams. Everything felt right and light.

At the headland, we found a flattish rock and sat and gazed into the ocean that felt not like the end, the death of the sun, but like an invitation to venture on. Returning later to the town beach, we watched as the tide washed up the shore and drew back, up and back, dissolving a footprint and offering a clean, smooth place for the next step. Rhythmically, the waves slid up the shore and drew back, up the shore and slipped back; the eternal pull that calls you out and then brings you safely home.